MW00989556

AGAINST THE TIDE

AGAINST THE TIDE

The best of Roger Scruton's columns,
commentaries and criticism

Roger Scruton

Edited by

Mark Dooley

BLOOMSBURY CONTINUUM
LONDON · OXFORD · NEW YORK · NEW DELHI · SYDNEY

BLOOMSBURY CONTINUUM
Bloomsbury Publishing Plc
50 Bedford Square, London, WC1B 3DP, UK
29 Earlsfort Terrace, Dublin 2, Ireland

BLOOMSBURY, BLOOMSBURY CONTINUUM and the Diana logo are trademarks
of Bloomsbury Publishing Plc

First published in Great Britain 2022

Copyright © The Estate of Roger Scruton, 2022
Preface © Mark Dooley, 2022

The Estate of Roger Scruton has asserted its right under the Copyright,
Designs and Patents Act, 1988, to be identified as Author of this work

All rights reserved. No part of this publication may be reproduced or transmitted in any form or
by any means, electronic or mechanical, including photocopying, recording, or any information
storage or retrieval system, without prior permission in writing from the publishers

Bloomsbury Publishing Plc does not have any control over, or responsibility for, any
third-party websites referred to or in this book. All internet addresses given in this
book were correct at the time of going to press. The author and publisher regret any
inconvenience caused if addresses have changed or sites have ceased to exist, but can
accept no responsibility for any such changes

A catalogue record for this book is available from the British Library

Library of Congress Cataloguing-in-Publication data has been applied for

ISBN: HB: 978-1-4729-9293-2; eBook: 978-1-4729-9292-5; ePDF: 978-1-4729-9291-8

2 4 6 8 10 9 7 5 3 1

Typeset by Deanta Global Publishing Services, Chennai, India
Printed and bound in Great Britain by CPI Group (UK) Ltd, Croydon CR0 4YY

MIX
Paper from
responsible sources
FSC® C171272

To find out more about our authors and books visit www.bloomsbury.com
and sign up for our newsletters

Contents

Preface: The Work That *Must* Be Done viii

PART ONE: WHO AM I? I

My Life Beyond the Pale 3
Roger Scruton Says 'Put a Cork in It' 8
My Week: July 2005 10
My Week: January 2006 13
My Week: April 2006 16
The Flame That Was Snuffed Out by Freedom 19
Finding *Scrutopia* in the Czech Republic 23
Diary – August 2016 26

PART TWO: WHO ARE WE? 29

The Conservative Conscience 31
The Blair Legacy 34
A Question of Temperament 37
The Meaning of Margaret Thatcher 42
Identity, Marriage, Family: Our Core Conservative Values
    Have Been Betrayed 50
What Trump Doesn't Get About Conservatism 54

PART THREE: WHY THE LEFT IS NEVER RIGHT 57

The Ideology of Human Rights 59
Who is a Fascist? 66
In Praise of Privilege 69
A Hominist Homily 72
In Loco Parentis 75

McCarthy Was Right on the Red Menace   79
A Focus of Loyalty Higher than the State   82
The Art of Taking Offence   85

PART FOUR: INTIMATIONS OF INFINITY   89
De Anima   91
A Matter of Life and Deathlessness   94
Dawkins Is Wrong about God   97
Altruism and Selfishness   101
Memo to Hawking: There's Still Room for God   106
Humans Hunger for the Sacred: Why Can't the
    New Atheists Understand That?   109

PART FIVE: THE END OF EDUCATION   113
The Virtue of Irrelevance   115
The Open University and the Closed Mind   118
The End of Education   121
The Plague of Sociology   124
Know Your Place   128
Universities' War against the Truth   133

PART SIX: FRAUDULENT PHILOSOPHY   137
A Note on Foucault   139
The Triumph of Nothingness   143
Freud and Fraud   146
If Only Chomsky Had Stuck to Syntax   149

PART SEVEN: THE WEST AND THE REST   153
In Memory of Iran   155
The Lesson of Lebanon   158
Decent Debate Mustn't Be the Victim   162
The Wrong Way to Treat President Putin   165
Why Iraq Is a Write-Off   168

PART EIGHT: CULTURAL CORRUPTION 173
The Art of Motor-Cycle Maintenance 175
Temples of Anxiety 178
The Modern Cult of Ugliness 181
High Culture Is Being Corrupted by a Culture of Fakes 185

PART NINE: ANIMAL RIGHTS, PULPIT POLITICS
    AND SEX 191
Male Domination 193
The Pestilence of Pulpit Politics 196
On the Eating of Fish 199
Obligations of the Flesh 202
Eat Animals! It's for Their Own Good 205
Sextants and Sexting 208
Tally Ho! Let the Hunt Remind Us of Who We Are 211

PART TEN: ANNUS HORRIBILIS AND LAST WORDS 215
Diary 217
After My Own Dark Night 220
My 2019 224

Index 233

Preface: The Work That *Must* Be Done

During our last conversation at his fabled Sunday Hill Farm in December 2019, Roger Scruton and I discussed many possibilities for future ventures: a sequel to our book *Conversations with Roger Scruton* (Bloomsbury, 2016), a series of online interviews for his YouTube channel and various conferences and seminars. Predominantly, however, our discussion focused on one important aspect of his work, and that was his journalism. After ten years I had recently ceased writing as a columnist for the *Irish Daily Mail*. When I remarked that it was a relief to be able to devote all my energy to writing about philosophical and spiritual matters again, Roger replied: 'Yes, I suppose it is, but writing about the issues that confront us is the work that *must* be done.'

Long before he published his first book in 1974, Scruton had featured in *The Spectator* magazine as a reviewer and critic. Indeed, a critical piece on the French philosopher Michel Foucault appeared in a 1971 edition of that publication and is included in this volume. However, it was when Charles Douglas-Home, the then editor of *The Times*, invited him to become a regular columnist, in 1983, that Scruton's name became central to the national conversation. Those columns, written over a four-year period, established Scruton as one of the greatest controversialists of the age. Speaking of them himself, he remarked that, while they 'scandalized the intellectual establishment', they nevertheless 'brought comfort to those of old-fashioned views'. They were 'frank expressions of unfashionable prejudice' which gave 'food for thought both to those who agree with them and to those who do not'.

Scruton's stint as a columnist for *The Times* ceased in 1986. By then he was known as a skilled writer who could tackle any subject with flair, intelligence and wit. Consequently, from that time to just before his death, he was rarely missing from the public conversation. This book is a testament to how widely respected he was as a journalist, his opinion pieces having featured in most major British and American newspapers. That is because, as he once wrote, the 'purpose of a newspaper column is neither to argue from first principles nor to engage in debate, but to present, as briefly as possible, a distinct point of view'. The fact that he could do so on almost any topic ensured that he was always sought by commissioning editors when an 'unfashionable opinion' needed to be expressed. However, his steadfast conviction was that 'opinions which are out of fashion may nonetheless be true'.

Addressing me as his literary executor during our last meeting, Scruton lamented that his early columns were no longer in circulation. This book attempts to redress that in as much as it contains a broad selection of his *Times* columns, but it goes much further in featuring pieces from the beginning to the end of his journalistic career. His having written so much on so many subjects, it was difficult for me to select what to include and what to omit. In the end, however, I believe this book honours Roger's wishes to have his journalism collected for posterity. Moreover, I am confident it will give readers a clear sense of Scruton's power as a writer and columnist, one whose view of the world was controversial yet so cleverly articulated that it often won praise even from his opponents.

At the age of 16 Scruton agonized over where he was going in life. Invariably, the answer would be: 'I must be a writer − that is the thing I *must* be.' He never thought about being an academic, let alone a philosopher. His calling was always to write poems, essays, novels, journalism and criticism. That he wrote, at a minimum, 500 words every day, proves how inexhaustible his ambition was to be not merely a writer but a *great writer*.

Scruton was a writer, a composer, a critic, a philosopher and, as I have said, a first-rate journalist. But, like everything else he wrote, his journalism was also a masterclass in literary precision. Consider these opening lines to a column he penned for *The Times* in 1984:

> Who remembers Iran? Who remembers, that is, the shameful stampede of Western journalists and intellectuals to the cause of the Iranian revolution? Who remembers the hysterical propaganda campaign waged against the Shah, the lurid press reports of corruption, police oppression, palace decadence, constitutional crisis? Who remembers the thousands of Iranian students in Western universities enthusiastically absorbing the fashionable Marxist nonsense purveyed to them by armchair radicals, so as one day to lead the campaign of riot and mendacity which preceded the Shah's downfall?

This is language used not merely to convey fact but to heighten tension, to unsettle and enrage. Each word is carefully chosen to assail the defences of his enemies and to stoke the righteous fury of those seeking truth over ideological fiction. It is enticing, provocative and scintillating. It is writing at its best.

'I must be a writer – that is the thing I *must* be.' And that is what Roger Scruton was: a man of letters who understood, like Hegel, that the intellectual life is ultimately a spiritual endeavour to synthesize art, music, religion, politics and philosophy. That Scruton achieved this with apparent ease belied the fact that he worked tirelessly to perfect every sentence he wrote. As he insisted in our book of conversations, 'craft really matters'. That, like every other truth he defended, was one he never betrayed. In showcasing his scope as a writer, scholar and journalist my hope is that this volume will secure Roger Scruton's place as a thinker who, like Bertrand Russell or George Orwell, never settled for the easy life when courage in defence of unpopular causes was demanded.

I would like to conclude by thanking my fellow executor of Sir Roger Scruton's literary estate, Sophie Scruton, for her support of this project, and for her guidance, advice and enduring friendship. I also owe deep gratitude to my friend and editor Robin Baird-Smith, whose unerring support and wisdom have ensured a much better book than originally conceived. Lastly, I wish to thank my eldest son, David, whose editorial assistance was invaluable.

Mark Dooley
Dublin
July 2021

PART ONE

Who Am I?

My Life Beyond the Pale

(*Spectator*, 2002)

It is 20 years since the Salisbury Group (a small gathering of old-fashioned Tories, informally chaired by the Marquess of Salisbury and dedicated to the political vision of his ancestor, the great prime minister) entrusted me with the task of establishing and editing a review, having raised £5,000 among themselves for this purpose. I had just published *The Meaning of Conservatism*, a somewhat Hegelian defence of Tory values in the face of their betrayal by the free marketeers. My credentials as an anachronism were therefore almost as good as the third Marquess's, and I took comfort in the fact that he, despite being opposed to the spirit of his age, had succeeded in imposing his mark on it, on and off, for 20 years.

The first difficulty was that of finding people to write in an explicitly conservative journal. I had friends in the academic world who were prepared in private to confess to conservative sympathies, but they were all acutely aware of the risks attached to 'coming out'. They had seen what a caning I had received for *The Meaning of Conservatism*, and few of them were far enough advanced in their academic careers to risk a similar treatment.

The second difficulty was that of establishing a readership. The money we had raised would cover the printing costs of three issues: after that the *Review* would have to pay for itself, which would require 600 subscribers or more. I was confident that there were at least 600 intellectual conservatives in Britain, most of whom would welcome a journal dedicated to expressing, examining and exploring their endangered worldview. The problem was finding them.

The third difficulty was that of conservatism itself. I was often told by Maurice Cowling (a member – though in a spirit of irony – of the Salisbury Group) that I was deceiving myself if I thought that conservative politics could be given a philosophical backing sufficient to put it on a par with socialism, liberalism, nationalism and all the other things that conservatism is not. Conservatism, Maurice told me, is a political practice, the legacy of a long tradition of pragmatic decision-making and high-toned contempt for human folly. To try to encapsulate it in a philosophy was the kind of quaint project that Americans might undertake. And that was one of the overwhelming reasons for not teaching, still less living, in America.

One of our earliest contributors was Ray Honeyford, the Bradford headmaster who argued for a policy of integration in our schools as the only way of averting ethnic conflict. Ray Honeyford was branded as a racist, horribly pilloried (by some of my academic colleagues in the University of Bradford, among others) and eventually sacked for saying what everyone now admits to be true. My attempts to defend him led to extensive libels of me and of the *Review*. Other contributors were persecuted (and also sometimes sacked) for coming to Ray's defence. This episode was our first great success, and led to the 600 subscriptions that we needed.

Our next success came in 1985, when, at the annual congress of the British Association for the Advancement of Science, the *Review* was subjected to a show trial by the sociologists and found guilty on the dual charge of 'scientific racism' and intellectual incompetence. Thereafter the *Review* and its writers were ostracized in the academic world. The consequences of this for my career soon became apparent. Invited to give a paper to the Philosophy Society in the University of Glasgow, I discovered, on arrival, that the philosophy department was mounting an official boycott of my talk, and had announced this fact to the world. I wandered around the campus for a while, watched a desultory procession of apparatchiks who were conferring an honorary degree on Robert Mugabe and was eventually rescued by a fellow dissident, Flint Schier, who had arranged for the talk to go ahead as an 'unofficial seminar'.

I was used to such things from Czechoslovakia, and in time got used to them in England too. On the whole, however, the communist secret police treated one rather better than the reception parties organized by the Socialist Workers Party: a slight roughing up and maybe a night in jail, but relieved by intellectual discussion at a much higher level than could be obtained in our provincial universities. After a particularly frightening experience giving a lecture on 'toleration' at the University of York, and following a libel in *The Observer* that made my position as a university professor untenable, I decided to abandon my academic career in Britain. *The Observer*, in its kindness, though under the instructions of a judge, paid for my early retirement.

Czechoslovakia was the occasion of another success. To my astonishment, a *samizdat* edition of the *Salisbury Review* began to appear in Prague in 1986. By then I had been expelled from Czechoslovakia, and was regularly followed in Poland. Things were not much better in Britain, where the *Review* might just as well have been a *samizdat* publication, so great was the venom directed towards those who wrote for it. So the news that the *Review* had achieved, under 'real socialism', an honour accorded, to my knowledge, to no other Western periodical was especially gratifying. Examples were smuggled to us, and their wafer-thin pages – the final carbon copies from sheaves of ten – had the spiritual quality of illuminated manuscripts. They were testimony to a belief in the written word that had been tried and proved by self-sacrificing labour.

In 1987 the Police Museum in Prague – a propaganda institute to which teachers would take their quiet crocodiles of 'young pioneers' – composed a new exhibition devoted to the 'unofficial secret agent'. The central item was a maquette of a youngish man in Western clothes, with spy camera and binoculars. From his open briefcase there spilled – along with Plato and Aristotle – copies of the *Salisbury Review*. Some time later, one of our regular contributors, Ján Čarnogurský, was arrested in Slovakia and charged with subversion of the state in collaboration with foreign powers. The indictment mentioned the *Salisbury Review* as clinching evidence. This was, I suppose, our greatest triumph: the first time that anybody with influence had conferred on us the status of an equal. Unfortunately, however, the trial never took place, with the communists out of power and Ján on his way to becoming prime minister of Slovakia.

It was not only the issues of race and national identity that had provoked the British intellectual establishment. The *Salisbury Review* was belligerently – and in my view intelligently – anti-communist; it took a stand against CND and the Peace Movement; it drew attention to the plight of Christians in North Africa and the Middle East; it carried articles denouncing foreign aid; it was explicitly critical of feminism, modernism, postmodernism and deconstruction. Above all, it was anti-egalitarian, defending achievement against mediocrity and virtue against vice. Although all those positions are now widely accepted, we had the good fortune to express them at a time when each was actively censored by some group of sanctimonious antis. Hence we survived. One by one the conservatives came out and joined us, recognizing that it was worth sacrificing your chances of becoming a fellow of the British Academy, a vice-chancellor or an emeritus professor for the sheer relief of uttering the truth. And although efforts to obtain funding were almost entirely unsuccessful, the dedicated work of our managing editor, Merrie Cave, whose home became a *samizdat* publishing house, ensured that we never got into debt.

With contributors ranging from Peter Bauer and A. L. Rowse to Václav Havel and P. D. James we were able to deflect the charge of intellectual incompetence. Without claiming too much credit for this, I remain convinced that the *Salisbury Review* helped a new generation of conservative intellectuals to emerge. At last it was possible to be a conservative and also to the *left* of something, to say, 'Of course the *Salisbury Review* is beyond the pale; but ...'. And, to my surprise and relief, one of these conservative intellectuals, the historian A. D. Harvey, showed himself both able and willing to take over as editor. Two years ago I was at last able to retire from a position that had cost me many thousand hours of unpaid labour, a hideous character assassination in *Private Eye*, three lawsuits, two interrogations, one expulsion, the loss of a university career in Britain, unendingly contemptuous reviews, Tory suspicion and the hatred of decent liberals everywhere. And it was worth it.

Roger Scruton Says 'Put a Cork in It'

(*New Statesman*, 2005)

Throughout life I have suffered from my cacophonous surname, now whispered into the pillows of Islington children so as to frighten them into their postmodern gender roles: 'Play with dolls, you wicked boy, or the Big Bad Scrute will get you.' It began at school, where I was 'Screwy' to the masses, 'Screwtape' to the literate and 'Screwtop' to those who wished to draw attention to the mound of red hair, the crowning defect of a creature whose unfitness for human society was apparent in his every tormented gesture. This does not lead me to look kindly on the screwtop bottle. But it does prompt reflection on the use and the beauty of corks.

To the naive observer, the cork is there to keep the wine in the bottle and the air out of it, with the result that 5 per cent of vintage wines are 'corked' – meaning spoiled by a defective stopper. To such an observer, the screwtop is the answer. I would respectfully retort that the risk of corking is essential to the ritual. The drinking of precious wine is preceded by an elaborate process of preparation, which has much in common with the ablutions that preceded ancient religious sacrifices. The bottle is retrieved from some secret place where the gods have kept it guarded; it is brought reverentially to the table, dusted off and uncorked with a slow and graceful movement while the guests watch in awed silence. The sudden 'pop' that then occurs is like a sacramental bell, marking a great division in the scheme of things, between a still life with bottle and the same still life with wine. The wine must then be swirled, sniffed and commented upon, and only when all this is duly accomplished can it be poured with ceremonial priestcraft into the glasses.

Wine properly served slows everything down, establishing a rhythm of gentle sips rather than gluttonous swiggings. The ceremony of the cork reminds us that good wine is not an ordinary thing, however often you drink it, but a visitor from a more exalted region and a catalyst of friendly ties. In short, thanks to the cork, wine stands aloof from the world of getting and spending, a moral resource that we conjure with a pop.

The screwtop has quite another meaning. It gives way at once, allowing no ritual of presentation and no sacramental sound effects. It deforms the bottle with metallic shards: imagine a still life with opened screwtop – impossible. It encourages the quick fix, the hasty glug, the purely self-centred grab for a slug of alcohol. It reduces wine to an alcopop and shapes it according to the needs of the drunkard. It reminds us of what we should lose, were the rituals of social drinking to be replaced by the mass loneliness of the binge-drinking culture. In short, there are no screwtops in Scrutopia.

My Week: July 2005

(previously unpublished)

Four musical performances in 48 hours combine to epitomize life in our privileged part of rural England. First *The Pepys Show*, presented by our children's school (Querns Westonbirt) of four- to eleven-year-olds, under the direction of the aptly named Mrs Gee – a teacher whose instinctive musicality is able to elicit song, dance and gesture from every child, and who introduces the show with Bach's Air on the G String. The parents stare open-mouthed at the spectacle, unable to believe that their offspring, whom they pack away each morning in the hope of hearing no more of them until four o'clock, spend their days in a world of historical imagination, reliving the Great Plague and the Fire of London, learning about the Crown of England, about the Restoration, the Court, the Puritans and other subjects banished from the state curriculum, and, what is more, encouraged to sing genuine melodies, harmonized in two parts or sung by the whole school in a three-part canon. We go away in stunned jubilation, praying that no spy had been present from Ofsted, Ofcom, Ofthewall or whatever the thought police are now called.

Ofthing would not have been pleased by our next appointment either. Leaving our children with Granny, we go across to the Beaufort Polo Club, where Mrs Georgie Fanshawe has organized a party to *Fight the Ban*. The hunt followers look as odd and carnivalesque without their uniforms as our children looked without theirs, though they lack the excuse that they are trying to resemble plague rats (an effect that hunt followers seem to achieve without the use of costumes). The marquee contains some 500 farmers, businessmen, landowners and yobs, and they exude a spirit of corporate defiance like that of wartime London, as portrayed by Ealing Studios.

Suddenly a corpulent singer called Riccardo (*sic*) leaps on to the stage. Were his voice not amplified to intolerable volume, his rendering of Kurt Weill's 'Mack the Knife' would have captured the mood. But he soon shows his colours as the cheesiest of Costa Brava crooners, interrupting himself to demand shrieks from the crowd, and continuing his ear-splitting declarations of love and desire until mercifully elbowed from the stage by a band of teenagers. How I longed, aged fourteen, to possess an electric bass guitar, and how interesting it is to see these talented young people, whose faces I dimly remember from the hunting field, playing their first gig, even if the repertoire has degenerated with the rise of Oasis, Blairitis and U2. It occurs to me that Ofthing should, after all, have been invited. The thought police might be more forgiving towards our community, on discovering that we are not toffs but proles.

Next evening we drive to Antonia Filmer's farm to eat our stoical picnics beneath a sky of threatening rain clouds. Here too there is a marquee, set up for a performance of *Don Giovanni*, in a cleverly reduced version by Nicholas Heath's portable Opera A La Carte. To the accompaniment of piano and wind quartet the singers move in the midst of the audience, turning a simple table, a few props and the air itself into a magical arena, where Colin Campbell's utterly believable Don proceeds proudly and inexorably to his doom. Mozart's combination of humour, moral seriousness and erotic immediacy – not to speak of melodic, harmonic and contrapuntal genius – make this opera into the most sublime of his masterpieces, and the conviction with which Rosalind Jones directs it from the piano communicates to the entire audience, even the hunt followers. The reduced forces suit the venue perfectly, and the result is a wonderful breath of fresh air.

Country life teaches that genuine recreation depends on women. This was true of the school *Pepys Show*, true of *Don*

Giovanni and true of the party in the polo club, which drew on that enormous reservoir of fundraising, child-minding, party-throwing and pony-club-organizing whereby women turn functional husbandry into a sense of belonging. No one in our community has done more in this respect than Elise Smith, founder of the Tetbury Music Festival, who has filled our houses, churches and village halls with real music. On her lawn the next day, fully expecting a Corelli concerto, I am amazed to discover The Cosmic Sausages, dressed in beachcomber casuals, swaying to their Neopolitan accompaniment of bass, mandolin, guitar and accordion. Among the assembled gentry they seem like out-of-work clowns in a Fellini film, and I give them a benign and pitying smile. At once they start forward, fall on their knees before me and begin a grotesquely corny serenade to the words 'La La!'. One thing about Elise is that you never know what she'll get up to next.

My Week: January 2006

(previously unpublished)

The time since Christmas has been spent in repossessing the farm – setting up tables and chairs in the half-finished kitchen, improvising Christmas decorations, digging up weeds, visiting neighbours, finding chickens to replace those taken by the fox and in general becoming one again with the mud, the damp and the benign, untroubled dreariness of England. Rural England is more populated and less splendid in its beauties than rural Virginia, where we have spent the autumn; but it has an intimacy and gentleness of its own, and the grey skies, washed-out fields and shadowy hedgerows retain a spiritual look that compensates, to some extent, for the almost total absence here of real religion. Of course, we sing carols at Christmas time, and on the day itself our church is full. But then it is all forgotten, the children are hidden behind their piles of toys like Freia behind the horde of Alberich, and we retire in a stupor to bed.

Life since Christmas has been one long battle with plastic. By a stroke of good fortune the toys given at Christmas had all broken by the new year: I explain to Sam and Lucy that this is what 'made in China' means, like 'made of China' when I was young. We pile them on the bonfire with the Christmas tree on top – the only Christmas ritual that fills me with joy. Then Sam and I take to the road, spending the new year holiday with our long-armed grabbers, cleaning up the verges from here to the top of our hill. This is a task that the local council – weighed down as it is with schemes to introduce diversity into the fire brigade and multiculturalism into the municipal swimming pool – can no longer afford to perform.

During the three months of our absence the ditches have filled to the brim with plastic. It is surely a vivid proof of the fact that we are no longer properly governed that the one simple remedy for environmental destruction – namely, the outlawing of non-degradable wrappings – is neither mooted in Parliament nor discussed by any of the Nosey Parker commissions established by the Eurocrats. Mrs Blair has once or twice hinted at the problem, but so far as I know she is unconnected to the government. As for the do-gooders and activists, they have been so busy trying to ensure that foxes are shot rather than hunted that they have neglected the most obvious problem, which is that, in a landscape as tightly wrapped in plastic as an installation by the Christos, there will be no foxes to shoot.

At last, the bank holidays are over. To London for a BBC interview on Islamic philosophy, which takes place in the wonderful exhibition devoted to the art of ancient Persia in the British Museum. We stand around saying inadequate things as our eyes wander in astonishment over the exhibits: fearful friezes in which identical slaves kowtow to an invisible monarch; lions eating horses, cup handles tormented into gazelles, countless cuneiform tablets and seals, a stamp of anonymous authority pressed on to every jar or bowl and not a human emotion to be had, not even in the presence of the woman in her bathtub of a tomb, her bones imprisoned in preposterous jewels, which were to bring her respect in the afterlife. It all seems like some trial run for the European Union. Mind you, when they dig up the remains of the Brussels empire they will find nothing much save plastic bottles, sandwich boxes and the occasional human form congealed in plastic. And, let's face it, the Middle East was better governed then than now.

Nor was it so well governed in the days of Avicenna, the eleventh-century philosopher who is the subject of our conversation. Vizier to tinpot sultans, he often had to flee for his life, leaving his manuscripts behind. Yet he sowed the seeds of the new Aristotelianism, put medicine on its modern path and shaped the Platonic theory of *eros* for its subsequent adoption by the poets of courtly love. He might have lived a little longer had he followed Plato's chaste example; instead he died, shagged out, aged 57. Even in his debilitated state, though, he was engaged at the time in besieging a city, pausing only to fortify himself with his habitual cup of wine. Reading his dry but orderly prose, in which all available learning parades in the distance like a back projection on the stage, you cannot help feeling the huge extent of Islam's subsequent decline. If only the ambition of the new satraps of the Middle East were to connect with their intellectual heritage, rather than with the technology of mass destruction. Looking round at the wreck of Ozymandias, however, I see how everything is programmed for destruction, and only the thoughts remain. Which is why we remember Avicenna, but not his tinpot sultans.

My Week: April 2006

(previously unpublished)

March this year has been as rainless in Virginia as in England. We return to parched meadows of sparse yellow grass, through which the river faintly trickles in a band of green slime. Winter storms have taken the caps off the chimneys and the gutters off the eves; old trees have fallen in heaps of splintered branches, and the flood plain is littered with the scattered remnants of our beaver dam. The skunk, the owls, the bobcat and the groundhog have all vanished, and in their place is a busy team of mice, who have found their way into the house and punctuated the kitchen with little black commas of crap.

The cows are hungry for the spring grass that has not come, and surround us expectantly when we walk through their field. Cows running wild lose all initiative, are unable to step forward from the herd and, while they long to smell you and to know you, will never risk a one-to-one encounter with a thing on two legs. Horses, by contrast, will come right up to you and sniff, processing the scent into their data bank before returning to the grass beneath their noses. Our neighbour's three hunters stand in a group in the centre of the field. They come across to us in a gentle swaying line, their tails swishing in the sunlight, their heads half raised to assess us.

A few streams still turgidly flow. The marshlands remain wet and full of quail, whistling up at our approach and then dropping into invisible hollows. Cloudy sacks of spawn bob in the brackish water; already the salamanders are hatching, and sentry-boxed crayfish hide in their banks. The locals take it all for granted, and I sadly reflect on our English experience, which tells me that people value wildlife only when it has been trampled, poisoned and persecuted until finally locked in the story book, never again to see the light of day.

The rain comes at last in a series of thunderstorms, sheet lightning tearing the darkness, huge drops clanging on the metal roof, thunderclaps shaking the walls and the children crying in terror on the wind-haunted staircase. The next day the rain persists, driven by a cold wind from the east, and winter returns. This is the day of the Old Dominion point-to-point, which takes place each year at Ben Venue, where there is a large grass arena overlooked by grassy knolls behind a colonial mansion. All Rappahannock County gathers here, not so much to watch the races, which occur in the background like softly thudding music at a party, as to invite each other to lavish feasts from the tailgates of their huge shining vehicles, perched on the slopes like the descended chariots of the gods. People gather under awnings whipped by gusts of cold wind. Roast pork and veal, fried chicken, asparagus, prawns, salmon and quiche – all the milk-and-honey abundance of America is there for the taking, offered for the joy of giving. The equestrian rationale is occasionally relayed from the loudspeaker, and the assembled crowd is glad of the reminder. For horses mean danger, danger means nerves and nerves mean whiskey. Soon they have drunk themselves another notch up the ladder of exultation.

For the sheer joy of being alive no place compares with rural America: not an Italian fiesta, not an African market, not a Hungarian round dance or a Scottish ceilidh, not even an English fox-hunt, radiates so much love of the earth and its fruits as an American rodeo or point-to-point. All enmities and rivalries are for this day set aside; all distinctions of class, learning, calling and politics are forgotten, and one thing alone is important, which is that we are here together now. Slight acquaintances rush towards each other with cries of unaffected pleasure, while families flow into families so that the children are suddenly shared.

A similar event in England would be dominated by the hunt, and imbued by a kind of retrospective melancholy as the season dwindles to a memory. In Virginia the hunt is also there, loudly announcing its right to exist with number plates saying 'tally-ho', 'gone away' or 'fox off'. But it provides only the skeleton to an event whose ample flesh is made of farmers, lawyers, real-estate agents, film-makers, teachers, writers, mechanics, pastors, shopkeepers and policemen. All mingle and salute each other, while above them there waves the flag of that quintessential American institution, the local volunteer rescue squad, the little platoon which parades on festive days, to which we are all invited and on which we all depend. And the flag reminds us that the wealth and security of America are no more durable than the public spirit of its people, and that if ever one day Americans ceased to volunteer for things, the show would be suddenly over.

The Flame That Was Snuffed Out by Freedom

(*The Times*, 2009)

For ten years before 1989 I was in the habit of visiting Eastern Europe to support the fragile underground educational networks there. I would meet my contacts on street corners at prearranged times, to be taken by tram to some smoke-filled room in an outlying apartment, where a group of whispering 'students' had gathered to meet me.

Every knock on the door was followed by a frozen silence, and from time to time someone would lift a corner of the curtain and peer anxiously into the street. Books in many languages lined the walls, and as often as not a crucifix would be fastened to the wall above the shelves.

The people I met were of many different casts of mind. Some among the older generation still maintained a belief in the 'socialism with a human face' that had been announced by Alexander Dubček, the Czechoslovak president, during the Prague Spring of 1968. Most of the younger people did not believe that socialism could wear a human face or that, if they tried to do so, it would look any better than one of those monsters with a human face painted by Hieronymus Bosch.

For the most part, the people I met were quiet, studious, often deeply religious, attempting to build shrines in the catacombs, around which small circles of marginalized people could gather to venerate the memory of their national culture. This was especially true of the Czechs, from whom their national culture had been officially confiscated after the Soviet invasion. In Poland and Hungary dissidents could still occupy posts in the official universities, and in Poland – after Pope John Paul II's pilgrimage to his homeland in 1979 – everyone was a dissident in any case. Still, that didn't alter the fact that there was a heavy price for opposing communism, and only a few were brave enough to pay it.

My small contribution consisted of joining like-minded colleagues to smuggle books and printing materials, to organize lectures and to maintain an underground messaging service. The experience taught me a lot about people, and in particular about the transforming effect of sacrifice on the human character. The people that I met were imbued with a more than ordinary gentleness and concern for one another. It was hard to earn their trust but, once offered, trust was complete.

Moreover, because learning, culture and the European spiritual heritage were, for them, symbols of their own inner freedom, and of the national independence they sought to remember, if not to regain, they looked on those things with unusual veneration. As a visitor from the world of fun, pop and comic strips, I was amazed to discover students for whom words devoted to such things were wasted words, and who sat in those little pockets of underground air studying Greek literature, German philosophy, medieval theology and the operas of Verdi and Wagner.

In 1985 the secret police moved against me and I was arrested in Brno; visits to Czechoslovakia came to an end, and I was followed in Poland and Hungary. But our team kept going until 1989, when, to our surprise, the catacombs were opened and our friends came pale, staggering and bewildered into the sunlight, to be hailed by the people as the natural trustees of their restituted country. This was a wonderful moment, and for a while I believed that the public spirit that had reigned in the catacombs would now govern the state.

It was not to be. Having been excluded for decades from the rewards of worldly advancement, our friends have failed to cultivate those arts – hypocrisy, treachery and *realpolitik* – without which it is impossible to stay in government.

They sat in their offices for a while, pityingly observed by their staff of former secret policemen, while affable and much-travelled rivals, of the kind with whom German Social Democrats and French Gaullists could both 'do business', carefully groomed themselves for the next elections.

Not since 1945 had so many records of party membership disappeared, or so many dissident biographies been invented. Within two years the real dissidents had returned to their studies, while the world outside was racing on, led by a new political class that had learned to add a record of outspoken dissidence to all its other dissimulations. We were witnessing what Dubček had promised: socialism with a human face.

The most urgent preoccupation of this new political class was to climb on to the European Union gravy train, which promised rewards of a kind that had been enjoyed, in previous years, only by the inner circle of the secret police.

The resistance we have seen to the EU in Eastern Europe should be understood in this light. Although incomparably more benign than the Communist Party, European institutions involve imposing top-down government, unaccountable offices and a system of elaborate rewards for co-operation on a people who all associate such things with the Soviet past. The Czechs, in particular, have been troubled to discover that the new political class prefers unanswerable imperial power to the ardours of accountable government. Only President Klaus, a survivor from those first days of jubilation, has tried to take a stand against the new Moloch, and he too has had to back down.

The Poles have been equally shocked by the impact of EU legislation that insists on 'non-discrimination' clauses and a battery of agenda-driven 'human rights' that conflict with fundamental tenets of the Catholic faith. For the ordinary voter it seems as if the Polish nation, whose claims had been celebrated every Sunday since Pope John Paul II's historic pilgrimage, has no part to play in the new political process. But in Poland too the political class is happy to be relieved of the burden of government by institutions that reward good behaviour and require no one to account for the really big decisions.

The EU has facilitated the transition away from communism. It has filled the legal vacuum – indeed, filled it to bursting. It has offered easy routes to cross-border trade and incoming investment. It has led to an exchange of expertise and – in Poland's case – to a mass escape of the working population.

But those countries today bear no resemblance to the liberated nations that were dreamed of in the catacombs. For, when the stones were lifted and the air of freedom blew across the underground altars, the flame that had been kept alive on them was instantly blown out.

Finding Scrutopia *in the Czech Republic*

(*Spectator*, 2013)

Haymaking was easy this year, and over in good time for a holiday. I am opposed to holidays, having worked all my life to build a sovereign territory from which departure will be a guaranteed disappointment. However, the children have yet to be convinced of the futility of human hopes, and therefore must be taken for a week or so to places that renew their trust in Scrutopia, as the only reliable refuge from an alien world. As always, we choose the Czech Republic; and as always, it disproves my point. I don't know what it is about Brno, but I am as at home there as I can be anywhere. And Sophie and the children feel the same.

We borrow the old cottage in the Moravian Sudetenland from which to explore a landscape wiped away by war. Since the expulsion of the Sudeten Germans, their fields have gradually reforested themselves. The lanes between the crops, in which every intersection was marked by a stone Calvary or a shrine to a patron saint, are now overgrown, the lovely statuary stolen for some bourgeois garden. And the churches, though still functioning thanks to an influx of Polish priests, have a neglected air, their colourful festivals no longer honoured, their old congregations remembered only in the German-language gravestones. Yet here, as elsewhere, the death of one way of life is the birth of another, and the depopulated landscape offers to the new generation of Czechs a perfect place for camping, fishing, swimming in lakes, cycling in family groups and in general reattaching themselves to their many times stolen country.

The contest over territory is a major stimulus to art, literature and music. To it we owe the great flowering of a national culture in the music of Janáček, in the writings of Hašek and Čapek, and in the little theatres that united the Czechs between the wars in a spirit of self-satire. This spirit still exists in Brno, thanks to the Theatre of the Goose on a String, run by the indefatigable Petr Oslzlý, who kept the thing going throughout the years of communist 'normalization', and who still sees it as a means of showing that nothing can ever be normalized if Czechs are involved. We spend a happy evening recalling our underground days, and wondering whether the Goose should mount a satire of the drunken President Zeman, or whether he is already satire enough.

Back home to discover that the chickens have not been eaten, the horses have not been kicked and the house is still standing. There is also a dog – another concession to the children and their incorrigible belief that there is always room for improvement. It is a border collie, a puppy, with an innate need to run after other animals and try to herd them into a corner. The horses ignore her, the cows turn on her menacingly, and the chickens fly squawking around the yard. Only with the fish are her efforts rewarded, since she runs around the edge of the pond as I feed them, and seems convinced that the fish are retained within its banks by her heroic efforts.

The best thing about summer is the Proms, and this year especially on account of Daniel Barenboim's wonderful performance of Wagner's Ring cycle. I have studied this stupendous work for most of my adult life, ever more convinced of its greatness and of the truth of its underlying vision. And in the passionate and deferential account given by Barenboim and his star-studded cast there could be no doubt about this. It was all the more persuasive for the absence of a producer, so that conductor and singers could devote themselves to the story, unimpeded by ludicrous sets. Why is it that we are now condemned to experience this work produced by one of the greatest imaginations that has ever existed, through the shrivelled imaginations of producers who know how to sneer at our ideals but have never understood why we need them?

One downside of the family holiday is that we miss the Proms performance of David Matthews's *A Vision of the Sea*. David celebrated his 70th birthday this year, and has established himself through constant hard work and ever-renewed inspiration as a leading exponent of symphonic form. He has continued to write beautiful music inspired by beautiful things in the teeth of the orthodox view that to be modern is to be challenging, disturbing, defiant, transgressive, etc., etc. The modernist advocacy of the defiant gesture has been far more productive of clichés and banalities than the attempt to go on writing as Beethoven wrote, 'from the heart, to the heart'. That attempt is still honoured in Britain, and the Proms bore witness to it with a brilliant performance by Vadim Repin of James MacMillan's melodious Violin Concerto. Would that the art establishment could learn from our composers that originality is not everything, and in any case not to be achieved by producing your own version of Duchamp's urinal.

Diary – August 2016

(*Spectator* 2016)

To Edinburgh for the book festival, where I am to explain my book *Fools, Frauds and Firebrands: Thinkers of the New Left* to respectable middle-class Scots, who have an endearing way of suggesting to me that I, like them, am a thing of the past. They queue to buy the book, which is nice of them; however, the publisher has failed to deliver any copies, so the need to part with a few quid for politeness's sake slips painlessly over the horizon. Only the students in the queue awaken me from my complacency. Where do we turn for comfort, they ask, when our reading lists are gibberish about which we can understand only that it is all left-wing? Is there no network, no secret society, no alternative reading list to get us through the next three years? Is there, in a modern university, no 'safe space' for conservatives?

I know of only one solution to leftist takeovers, and that is to start again. The decent parliamentarians in the Labour Party should take note of this. When we set up the underground university in Prague, we composed a curriculum entirely of classics on a budget of £50,000 a year. We the teachers, and they the students, were volunteers; our shared concern was knowledge, not ideology; conversation, not conscription. Once the state takes over, however, and its vast resources are made available to people otherwise incapable of earning a penny, the fakes and the frauds muscle in. Chanting gobbledegook from Deleuze confers an air of erudition on even the most second-rate intellect, and since in most humanities departments teaching is no longer required and the only tests are political, there is no answer to those desperate students except to start something new. That is what we are doing at the University of Buckingham.

Back home to a punishing hour of physiotherapy. Two surprising and wonderful things happened to me this year. The first was a fall from a bridge, on my horse Desmond — who broke my femur in four places while using it to lever himself out of the water. That was five months ago, and the rescue by air ambulance and the NHS filled me with a kind of gratitude I hardly knew. The slow recovery has been a time to think about what matters to me, and how other people matter more. Even physiotherapy, with those thoughts in mind, is welcome.

The second surprising and wonderful thing was the knighthood conferred in the Queen's birthday honours list, not for my services to righteous indignation (proud though I am of them) but for my life as an educator. At the very moment when my wife, Sophie, as a master of foxhounds at the VWH Hunt, has earned those precious letters 'MFH' after her name, she can now put 'Lady' in front of it. A pity, of course, that the name is mine, with its ludicrous sound, so easily satirized. But you can't have everything, and in any case, euphonious though her maiden name of Jeffreys might be, she must live with the fact that she inherited it from the most notorious hanging judge in English history.

Of course, in the first-name culture that now prevails, titles might seem merely decorative, and offensive to the cult of equality. The death of the Duke of Westminster has briefly raised the question of what a titled aristocracy does for us. My own view is that titles are much to be preferred to wealth as a mark of distinction, since they give glamour without power. They promote the idea of purely immaterial reward, and represent eminence as something to live up to, not a power to be used. Of course they can be abused, and a kind of snobbery goes with them. Take them away, however, and you have the mean-minded obsessions of 'celebrity' culture, the American idolization of wealth or the power cult of the Russian mafia. An inherited title sanctifies a family and its ancient territory. The poetry of this is beautifully expressed by Proust, who wrote of an aristocracy from which everything had been taken except its titles – think of 'Guermantes' and compare it with 'Trump'.

Back home in my role as grand panjandrum of Horsell's Farm Enterprises, and preparing for Apple Day on 22 October, to which you are all invited. Our business is a terrific wheeze which brings together all the things we do on a single patch of earth and brands them with the coveted name of 'farming'. We have even managed to assemble a group of stray conservatives for a conference in nearby Cirencester as part of our mission to foster worldwide dissent. They (the Vanenburg Meeting) are youngish, come from all parts of Western civilization and agree about one thing only, which is the right of that civilization to defend itself. And everything I see from my window, cows included, confirms what they believe.

PART TWO

Who Are We?

The Conservative Conscience

(*Salisbury Review*, 1994)

We live in troubling times for the conservative conscience. The West is adrift without leadership, anarchy is spreading through Asia and Africa, and the political process in Europe has been absorbed by the fantasy of European union. Almost everywhere in the civilized world we encounter the signs of social decay: the decline in religious observance and local customs; the rise of crime and violence; the pornocratic culture of the mass media; the desecration of love and marriage; the collapse of education and the retreat of the individual into his private pleasure dome. These things threaten to populate the world with a new human species – cold-hearted, disloyal, promiscuous, uncultured and godless – whose sole pursuit is present pleasure, and who looks on the sufferings of others with indifference or delight. In the face of this prospect those of us who were brought up in the old dispensation might be tempted to despair and the more so when we see how many of our own generation are prepared to accept or justify the reigning trivialities, and to preach the forward-looking gospel that sees nothing to be criticized in women priests, Sir Richard Rogers or the new Radio 3.

Cultural despair has been with us, however, for many decades, and writers who have no other message, or who seek to comfort us with fantasies of a life outside civilization, merely illustrate what they condemn. The exasperated writings of men like F. R. Leavis and D. H. Lawrence are also exasperating. We live only once, and that once is *now*. The choice lies before us, as it has lain before every human being in history, to live well or badly, to be virtuous or vicious, to love or to hate. And this is an *individual* choice, which depends on cultural conditions only obliquely, and which no other person can make in our stead. If our culture is demoralized, it is in part for want of good examples. A good neighbour, loving parent, conscientious teacher, loyal friend or faithful spouse is an object not only of admiration but of emulation too. Nobody likes, still less admires, coldness, idleness or infidelity, even when he finds these qualities in himself. It is in our nature as social and moral beings to be drawn to virtue and repelled by vice, and society can never degenerate to the point where vice alone has a following. By living well we help others to live well, and this is a source of joy for us and for them.

Indeed, if we were to view the matter *sub specie aeternitatis,* we might be persuaded that it is good to have been born in this time of decay. Our generation was granted a privilege that future generations may never know – a view of Western civilization in its totality, and a knowledge of its inner meaning. We were given the pure truths of the Christian religion, and the morality of sacrifice which turns renunciation into triumph and suffering into a secret joy. We also had the chance to see what will happen, should we lose these gifts. We had an opportunity to work on their behalf that no previous generation has been granted, and which no future generation may desire.

If our political leaders disappoint us, it is either because they have no inkling of this opportunity, or because they regard it with the kind of bored cynicism that prevents them from setting an example. But there is more to life than politics, and even those who lack the deep restfulness that comes from true religion may still find themselves surprised by joy. For consider what has *not* been destroyed: music, poetry and art; the sacred texts and the secular knowledge that derives from them; the impulse to love and to learn, which will vanish only with the human species; the still-warm habit of association and institution-building, into which all our better impulses may feed. These are the counters to despair, and the source of hope in any age. Society depends on the saints and heroes who can once again place these things before us and show us their worth. This is not a task for the politician, whose proper role is not to create a society but rather to represent it. It is a task for the educator, the priest and the ordinary citizen whose public spirit is aroused on behalf of his neighbours.

Such people are reluctant to come forward, largely because the mass media, dominated by trivializing materialists and sarcastic cynics, will cover them with ridicule. But the great merit of our civilization, and of the Christian religion on which it is founded, is that it teaches us to accept ridicule, to know that the best is always mocked by that which feels condemned by it and to take comfort in handing on knowledge to *one* person, regardless of the scorn of those who could never receive it in any case. Of course, it is hard to feel the full confidence that those teachings require. But they are addressed to each of us individually, and their validity is not affected by what others think or do. We have within ourselves the source of our salvation: all that is needed is to summon it, and to go out into the world.

The Blair Legacy

(*Salisbury Review*, 1997)

What will be the most lasting effect of Mr Blair's government? Will it be massive constitutional change, the consolidation of the European power structure, the ruin of private education or the growth of a new quangocracy? Or will it be something else, some hitherto unimagined innovation, fitting testimony to a socialist party that has discarded the socialist agenda while acquiring no other to replace it? The nation waits with bated breath for the real deeds that will give meaning to so many unreal words. But the nation should not forget the words, for New Labour is the product of chatter. Its policies – such as the proposals for constitutional reform – are ventures into reality from the armchair. They have the unreal air of common-room debates, in which, however, only one side is heard.

And this will be the most important effect of Mr Blair in power: the triumph of political correctness. Policies will be chosen not for their prudence or because there is a need for them. They will be chosen in order to advance the culture of equality and inclusion, the culture of our universities, which is now about to break out into the world of real decision-making. Whether or not affirmative action is introduced over here, it is certain that the American feminist conception of women, of the family and of employment will gain a hearing. Lawsuits for sexual and racial discrimination will increase, and victim status will become universally coveted. New classes of victims will be discovered by the week. At the end of this Parliament everyone in Britain will be a victim, apart from the minority of hard-working, over-taxed, middle-class males who bear the cost of the remainder.

The breakdown of the traditional family will continue, and new reproductive strategies will emerge to replace it. *In vitro* fertilization will be available on the NHS, with preference given to lesbians. Family ties will be increasingly penalized by the tax system, as will all attempts to educate one's children privately. The moronization of the school curriculum will continue, and pseudo-subjects like media studies, communication studies, social studies, sports studies, women's studies, race and gender studies; in brief, for any politically correct *x, x*-studies will become the norm in universities. Modular assessment will replace final exams, and single-subject degrees will disappear. The tutorial system will be abolished, and Oxford and Cambridge colleges will eagerly strive to show their correctness, by lowering the admission standard for pupils from state comprehensives and raising it for those from public schools.

Honours will be awarded to pop stars, cultural postmodernists and the milkers of the 'voluntary sector', with special emphasis on minorities. The BBC will be given over to egalitarian propaganda, and all attempts to distinguish 'high-brow' from 'low-brow' entertainment will be finally abandoned. Meanwhile the position of the salon socialist establishment will be consolidated in all the major cultural institutions. The modernist clique will remain in charge of the Royal Academy; the art galleries will be run by clones of Michael Craig-Martin and Damien Hirst; the British Academy will be controlled by the left-liberal protégés of Sir Isaiah Berlin, and the planning of the New Britain will be entrusted to Lord Rogers of Riverside. Vice-chancellors will be dull progressives with backgrounds in engineering or soil science, while the important advisory bodies will be composed of political activists from local government, with a track record in anti-racist, anti-sexist, anti-nuclear, anti-homophobic and other forms of anti-bourgeois agitation.

The ideology of equality and rights will replace that of reward and duty, and the edicts of the European courts will gradually extinguish the old common-law idea of individual responsibility. 'Group rights' will be recognized and enforced by the courts and built into legislation, with favoured minorities obtaining privileges denied to any ethnic Anglo-Saxon. Titles and forms of address will disappear, subjects will become 'citizens' and no name will be used in public discourse apart from the first name – no longer called 'Christian' since that would discriminate against Muslims, pagans and Jews.

Culture and education will be increasingly regarded as dangerous, and efforts will be made, especially in schools, to ensure that the genuinely educated never obtain an opportunity to teach. Even as government of the nation's affairs is transferred to foreign bureaucrats, fewer and fewer British 'citizens' will be able to read or speak any language but their own. Their grasp of English will also decline, as imperfect grammar and improvised vocabulary acquire the status of legitimate 'alternatives'.

Sexual laxity will become official government policy, with condoms and abortions freely available to children at any age. Sex advisers will prowl the schools in search of innocence, in order to destroy it, and new codes of ethics will be introduced in the place of religion – codes that no longer 'privilege' marriage or heterosexual union over the equally legitimate alternatives. Meanwhile young offenders will be placed in the hands of leftist probation officers, who would help them back on to their feet, and into the pockets of their middle-class victims, while joyriding will be legitimized as an authentic expression of the frustrations of the young.

In short, everything will proceed as it has done under the Tories, only faster, and without the damaging residue of guilt.

A Question of Temperament

(*Wall Street Journal*, 2002)

Here and there in the modern world you can find countries with conservative parties. Britain is one of them. But the US is the last remaining country with a genuine conservative movement. This conservative movement is expressed in politics, in social initiatives among ordinary people, in the media and in intellectual journals with an explicitly conservative message. True, political philosophy in the American academy has been dominated by liberals, and by the project to which the late John Rawls devoted his life, of producing a theory of justice that would vindicate the welfare state. Nevertheless, even in American universities you can come across conservatives who are prepared to defend their beliefs.

In Britain there are very few academics who will publicly confess to conservative convictions. And we have only two noteworthy conservative journals: the weekly *Spectator*, and the quarterly *Salisbury Review*, which I edited (at enormous cost to my intellectual career) for its first 18 years of life, and whose tiny circulation is maintained almost exclusively by private subscription. In the US, by contrast, conservative journals spring up constantly, find large and sympathetic readerships and frequently attract funding from foundations and business. Yet another conservative journal has appeared recently, and the high profile of its editor – Patrick Buchanan – will lead to much speculation about what is really meant by the journal's name: *American Conservative*. Maybe a British conservative can cast a little light on this.

It is a tautology to say that a conservative is a person who wants to conserve things: the question is what things? To this I think we can give a simple one-word answer: *us*. At the heart of every conservative endeavour is the effort to conserve a historically given community. In any conflict the conservative is the one who sides with 'us' against 'them' – not knowing but trusting. He is the one who looks for the good in the institutions, customs and habits that he has inherited. He is the one who seeks to defend and perpetuate an instinctive sense of loyalty, and who is therefore suspicious of experiments and innovations that put loyalty at risk.

So defined, conservatism is less a philosophy than a temperament; but it is, I believe, a temperament that emerges naturally from the experience of society, and which is indeed necessary if societies are to endure. The conservative strives to diminish social entropy. The second law of thermodynamics implies that, in the long run, all conservatism must fail. But the same is true of life itself, and conservatism might equally be defined as the social organism's will to live.

Of course, there are people without the conservative temperament. There are the radicals and innovators, who are impatient with the debris left by the dead; and their temperament too is a necessary ingredient in any healthy social mix. There are also the instinctive rebels of the Chomsky variety, who in every conflict side with 'them' against 'us', who scoff at the ordinary loyalties of ordinary people and who look primarily for what is bad in the institutions, customs and habits that define their historical community. Still, by and large, the future of any society depends on the solid residue of conservative sentiment, which forms the ballast to every innovation, and the equilibrating process that makes innovation possible.

September 11, 2001, raised the question 'Who are we, that they should attack us, and what justifies our existence as a "we"?' American conservatism is an answer to that question. 'We the people', it says, constitute a nation, settled in a common territory under a common rule of law, bound by a single constitution and a common language and culture. Our primary loyalty is to this nation, and to the secular and territorially based jurisdiction that makes it possible for our nation to endure. Our national loyalty is inclusive and can be extended to newcomers, but only if they assume the duties and responsibilities, as well as the rights, of citizenship. And it is reinforced by customs and habits that have their origin in the Judaeo-Christian inheritance, and which must be constantly refreshed from that source if they are to endure. In the modern context the American conservative is an opponent of 'multiculturalism', and of the liberal attempt to sever the constitution from the religious and cultural inheritance that first created it.

American conservatism welcomes enterprise, freedom and risk, and sees the bureaucratic state as the great corrupter of these goods. But its philosophy is not founded in economic theories. If conservatives favour the free market, it is not because market solutions are the most efficient ways of distributing resources – although they are – but because they compel people to bear the costs of their own actions, and to become responsible citizens. Conservative reservations about the welfare state reflect the belief that welfare generates a dependency culture, in which responsibilities are drowned by rights.

The habit of claiming without earning is not confined only to the welfare machine. One of the most important conservative causes in America must surely be the reform of the jury system, which has allowed class actions and frivolous claims – including claims by non-nationals – to sabotage the culture of honest reward, and to ensure that wealth, however honestly and diligently acquired, can at any moment be stolen from its producer to end up in the pocket of someone who has done nothing to deserve it.

It is one of the great merits of America's conservative movement that it has seen the need to define its philosophy at the highest intellectual level. British conservatism has always been suspicious of ideas, and the only great modern conservative thinker in my country who has tried to disseminate his ideas through a journal – T. S. Eliot – was in fact an American. The title of his journal (*The Criterion*) was borrowed by Hilton Kramer when he founded what is surely the only contemporary conservative journal that is devoted entirely to ideas. Under the editorship of Mr Kramer and Roger Kimball, *The New Criterion* has tried to break the cultural monopoly of the liberal establishment, and is consequently read in our British universities with amazement, anger and (I like to think) self-doubt.

Eliot's influence has been spread in America by his disciple Russell Kirk, who made clear to a whole generation that conservatism is not an economic but a cultural outlook, and that it would have no future if reduced merely to the philosophy of profit. Put bluntly, conservatism is not about profit but about loss: it survives and flourishes because people are in the habit of mourning their losses, and resolving to safeguard against them. This does not mean that conservatives are pessimists. In America they are the only true optimists, since they are the only ones with a clear vision of the future and a clear determination to bring that future into being.

For the conservative temperament, the future is the past. Hence, like the past, it is knowable and lovable. It follows that by studying the past of America – its traditions of enterprise, risk-taking, fortitude, piety and responsible citizenship – you can derive the best case for its future: a future in which the national loyalty will endure, holding things together, and providing all of us, liberals included, with our required sources of hope. This is the message that has been put across vividly by New York's *City Journal*, and it is interesting to compare its optimistic articles about the American underclass with the bleak vision of our English equivalent expressed in the same journal by Theodore Dalrymple.

September 11 was a wake-up call through which liberals have managed to go on dreaming. American conservatives ought to seize the opportunity to utter those difficult truths which have been censored out of recent debate: truths about national loyalty, about common culture and about the duties of citizenship. You never know, Middle America might actually recognize itself at last, when addressed in this way.

The Meaning of Margaret Thatcher

(*The Times*, 2013)

For politicians on the left, 'patriotism' had become a dirty word, more or less synonymous with 'racism'. For politicians on the right, nothing seemed to matter, save the rush to be a part of the new Europe, whose markets would protect us from the worst effects of post-war stagnation. The national interest had been displaced by vested interests: by the unions, the establishments and the 'captains of industry'.

The situation was especially discouraging for conservatives. For Edward Heath, their nominal leader, believed that to govern is to surrender: we were to surrender the economy to the managers, the education system to the socialists and sovereignty to Europe. The old guard of the Tory Party largely agreed with him, and had joined in the scapegoating of Enoch Powell, the only one among them who had publicly dissented from the post-war consensus. In the bleak years of the 1970s, when a culture of repudiation spread through the universities and the opinion-forming elites, it seemed that there was no way back to the great country that had successfully defended our civilization in two world wars.

Then, in the midst of our discouragement, Margaret Thatcher appeared, as though by a miracle, at the head of the Conservative Party. I well remember the joy that spread through the University of London, where I was teaching. At last there was someone to hate! After all those dreary years of socialist consensus, poking in the drab corners of British society for the dingy fascists and racists who were the best that could be found by way of an enemy, a real demon had come on the scene: a leader of the Tory Party, no less, who had the effrontery to declare her commitment to the market economy, private enterprise, the freedom of the individual, national sovereignty and the rule of law – in short, to all the things that Marx had dismissed as 'bourgeois ideology'. And the surprise was that she did not mind being hated by the Left, that she gave as good as she got and was able to carry the people with her.

She encouraged the electorate to recognize that the individual's life is his own and that the responsibility of living it cannot be borne by anyone else, still less by the state. She set out to release the talent and enterprise that, notwithstanding decades of egalitarian claptrap, she believed yet to exist in British society. The situation she inherited was typified by the National Economic Development Council, set up under a lame Conservative government in 1962, in order to manage the country's economic decline. Staffed by bigwigs from industry and the civil service, 'Neddy', as it was known, devoted itself to perpetuating the illusion that the country was in 'safe hands', that there was a plan, that managers, politicians and union leaders were in it together and working for the common good. It epitomized the old British establishment, which addressed the nation's problems by appointing committees of the people who had caused them. Its ruling idea was that economic life consists in the management of existing industries, and not in the creation of new ones. Wilson, Heath and Callaghan had all relied on Neddy to confirm their shared belief that, if you held on long enough, things would come out OK and any blame would fall on your successor. By contrast, Margaret Thatcher believed that, in business as in politics, the buck stops here. The important person in a free economy is not the manager but the entrepreneur – the one who takes risks and meets the cost of them. Entrepreneurs create things; managers entomb them: so she taught us, and it was immediately apparent that she was right, since the effects of the management culture lay all around us.

I say it was immediately apparent, but it was not apparent to the intellectual class, which has remained largely wedded to the post-war consensus to this day. The idea of the state as a benign father figure, who guides the collective assets of society to the place where they are needed, and who is always there to rescue us from poverty, ill-health or unemployment, has remained in the foreground of academic political science in Britain. Only this morning, preparing a lecture in political philosophy, I was interested to discover that the prescribed text describes something called the New Right, associated by the author with Thatcher and Reagan, as a radical assault on the vulnerable members of society. The author's argument is devoted to the distribution of wealth, on the assumption that this is the main task of government and that government is uniquely competent to embark on it. The fact that wealth can be distributed only if it is first created seems to have escaped his notice. ✓

To set about creating wealth, Margaret Thatcher had first to break the power of the unions, which meant confronting Stalinists like Arthur Scargill. That great conflict was only one of many. Perhaps the most important lesson to be learned from her political style is that negotiation and compromise may sometimes be right, but that confrontation and defiance are just as important, and sometimes the only resource. She understood the damage that had been done to our country throughout the twentieth century by the policy of appeasement. And when the opportunity came to choose confrontation instead, she immediately and instinctively grasped it. Her decision to resist the junta of fascist generals who had seized power in Argentina recalled Queen Elizabeth I confronting King Philip of Spain. The Falklands War restored our national pride, and strengthened Thatcher's resolve to counter the Soviet menace. It also gave her the authority to confront the IRA and to show the Republican movement that terrorist tactics would not succeed.

Lady Thatcher's ambitions went far beyond her unaided capacity to achieve them. She hoped to reform the education system, opposing the socialist apparatchiks who control it and holding up their 'progressive' curriculum to scorn. But she had no policy that could possibly defeat them, and education remains a socialist fiefdom to this day, notwithstanding Michael Gove's brave attempts to reform it. She would have liked to take on the welfare state itself, and to persuade people that their lives could be better, freer and simpler if the welfare system belonged to them and not to the bureaucrats. But you cannot take on vested interests without making yourself hated, and you cannot enjoy the support of the ordinary middle-class voter without arousing the anger of the intellectuals, who dislike nothing so much as the ordinary middle-class voter. Regular letters would appear in *The Times*, signed by the great and the good of the day, denouncing this or that policy of her government as the prelude to irreversible disaster. Proposed for an honorary doctorate at her *alma mater*, Oxford University, she was resoundingly voted down by a Convocation that was not impressed by her standing as Britain's first woman prime minister. The vote called to mind that of the Oxford Union in 1933, when the motion that 'this House will in no circumstances fight for its King and country' was carried by a large majority. On both occasions Oxford showed how little our intellectual establishment has in common with the British people.

Of course, Thatcher was not an intellectual, and was motivated more by instinct than by a properly worked-out philosophy. As *The Times* editorial put it, on the day after her death, she was a 'woman of simple truths'. Pressed for arguments, she leaned too readily on market economics, and ignored the deeper roots of conservatism in the theory and practice of civil society. Her passing remark that 'there is no such thing as society' was gleefully seized on by my university colleagues as proof of her crass individualism, her ignorance of social philosophy and her allegiance to the values of the new generation of businessmen, which could be summarized in three words: money, money, money. Actually what Thatcher meant on that occasion was quite true, though the opposite of what she said. She meant that there is such a thing as society, but that society is not identical with the state. Society is composed of people, freely associating, and forming communities of interest that socialists have no right to control, and no authority to subject to their obsessions.

To express it in that way, however, was not Thatcher's style and not what her followers expected of her. What the British public wanted, and what they got, was the kind of instinctive politician whom they could see at once to be speaking for the nation, whether or not she had the right fund of abstract arguments. She spoke simply and intelligibly of freedom and enterprise. But, as Charles Moore pointed out in his delicate and perceptive tribute in the *Daily Telegraph*, she was convinced that the rule of law was more important than either of those things, since without it they could not endure. She saw the law of our country as deeply entwined with our national history, and as defining a unique and precious perspective on the world.

Of course, she felt the winds of intellectual scorn that blew around her, and sheltered behind a praetorian guard of economic advisers versed in 'market solutions', 'supply-side economics', 'consumer sovereignty' and the rest. But those fashionable slogans did not capture her core beliefs. All her most important speeches as well as her enduring policies stemmed from a consciousness of national loyalty. She believed in our country and its institutions, and saw them as the embodiment of social affections nurtured and stored over centuries. Family, civil association, the Christian religion and the common law were all integrated into her ideal of freedom under law. And in her judgement that was the cause for which our country had stood up in the past and must stand up in the future.

Lady Thatcher so changed things that it became impossible for the Labour Party to wrap itself again in its Victorian cobwebs: Clause IV (the commitment to a socialist economy) was dropped from its constitution, and a new middle-class party emerged, retaining nothing of the old agenda apart from the desire to punish the upper class, and the odd belief that the way to do this is by banning fox-hunting. At the time, however, it was not Thatcher's impact on domestic policy that was most vividly felt but her presence on the international stage. Her commitment to the Atlantic alliance, and preparedness to stand side by side with President Reagan in defiance of the Soviet threat, entirely changed the atmosphere in Eastern Europe. Quite suddenly, people who had been broken and subdued by the totalitarian routine learned that there were Western leaders who were prepared to press for their liberation. John O'Sullivan has forcefully argued that the simultaneous presence in the highest offices of Reagan, Thatcher and Pope John Paul II was the cause of the Soviet collapse, and my own experience confirms this. Working with underground networks in the communist states, I learned that Eastern Europeans of my generation were not merely disillusioned with communism. They had discovered that capitalism – the bogeyman of all the communist fairy-tales – was real, positive and believable. If Mrs Thatcher and President Reagan believed in it, then they would believe in it too. And their eagerness to learn about capitalism was a great inspiration to me in those days when the subject was all but taboo in my university.

Lady Thatcher's foreign policy initiatives were not to everyone's liking. As far as I could see, the Foreign Office had no desire to rock the boat when it came to the post-war division of Europe; it was not until her minister for Eastern Europe, Malcolm Rifkind, visited the grave of the martyred Father Popiełuszko in Poland that any official recognition was extended to the Polish opposition, and Rifkind's gesture was not, I believe, sanctioned by the Foreign Office. But afterwards everything in Poland changed. The point had been made that the Communist Party was not the legitimate government of Poland, and that the ground must now be prepared for its successor.

Likewise, when it came to dealing with international terrorism, the British establishment took radically against Thatcher's instinct, which was not to negotiate but to punish. When, following proof of Syrian involvement in the attempt to blow up an El-Al airliner flying from Heathrow, she broke off diplomatic relations with Syria, our ex-ambassador to that country, speaking for the Foreign Office establishment, publicly condemned the move as exactly the wrong way to deal with the nice President Hafez al-Assad. I happened to be in Lebanon at the time, when Syrian troops were fomenting civil war on the pretence of containing it, and our leftist journalists were making propaganda on behalf of Assad. Almost everyone I met told me that, thanks to Mrs Thatcher, they had experienced a moment of hope – a moment when it was possible to believe that their fragile democracy would not after all be sacrificed to the mad ambitions of the Assad family. It was none of Lady Thatcher's doing that their hopes were to be dashed.

Looking back on it, I should say that Thatcher's greatest legacy was to have placed the nation and the national interest at the centre of politics. She never succeeded in her most important task, which was to negotiate the return of our sovereignty from Europe. I suspect that she did not see clearly enough that the European process, as constituted by the treaties, authorizes the unresisted conquest of our country and the confiscation of our national assets. In the anxiety that this thought arouses in me I can only regret, for the thousandth time, that she was finally rejected by the party whose fortunes she revived. Why did it happen?

Of course, she was confrontational; she made enemies in places where she might have made friends. By threatening the culture of state dependency she rocked the Establishment that had been built on it: the BBC, the universities, the schools, the socialist quangos, the welfare services, the vast heap of civil servants. But why was she rejected by the Tory Party? I am reminded of the Athenian general Themistocles. It was he who had created the Athenian navy, held the Persians at Artemisium and finally defeated them at Salamis. It was he who had fortified Athens and made it the most prosperous city of the Aegean. But in 471 BC he was ostracized and sent into exile. His work was continued by Pericles, without whose energy and public spirit the democratic traditions of Athens would certainly have been destroyed.

But Pericles also was driven from office, tried on trumped-up charges and threatened with exile.

It seems that democracies have a natural tendency to turn against their saviours. It happened to Winston Churchill. It happened to Charles de Gaulle, and it happened to Margaret Thatcher. It was not the faults of those great leaders that caused their downfall but their virtues. Thatcher, like Themistocles, was overthrown by the resentment of her inferiors. For in a democracy such people have power. Now that she has gone from us, however, and no longer poses a threat to all the ambitions that her presence once obstructed, she will surely be acknowledged, even by those who conspired to remove her, as the greatest woman in British politics since Queen Elizabeth I.

Identity, Marriage, Family: Our Core Conservative Values Have Been Betrayed

(*Guardian*, 2013)

The important lesson of the local elections is not that the Conservative Party is losing appeal for marginal groups and floating voters – to whom it never appeals for long in any case. The important lesson is that the party has jeopardized the allegiance of its core constituents, those who willingly describe themselves as conservatives and live according to the unspoken norms of a shared way of life.

Such people are not all middle-class, not all prosperous, not all brought up to think that economics is the only thing that matters. When politicians address them with questions such as 'How do we repair the economy?', 'How do we reform our educational system?' or 'How do we ensure a fair deal for pensioners?' there is one word that stands out for them, and that word is 'we'. Who are we, what holds us together, and how do we stay together so as to bear our burdens as a community? For conservatism is about national identity. It is only in the context of a first-person plural that the questions – economic questions included – make sense, or open themselves to democratic argument.

Such was the idea that Edmund Burke tried to spell out 200 years ago. Burke was a great writer, a profound thinker and a high-ranking political practitioner, with a keen sense of both the damage done by the wrong ideas and the real need for the right ones. Political wisdom, Burke argued, is not contained in a single head. It does not reside in the plans and schemes of the political class, and can never be reduced to a system. It resides in the social organism as a whole, in the myriad small compromises, in the local negotiations and trusts, through which people adjust to the presence of their neighbours and co-operate in safeguarding what they share. People must be free to associate, to form 'little platoons', to dispose of their labour, their property and their affections, according to their own desires and needs.

But no freedom is absolute, and all must be qualified for the common good. Until subject to a rule of law, freedom is merely 'the dust and powder of individuality'. But a rule of law requires a shared allegiance, by which people entrust their collective destiny to sovereign institutions that can speak and decide in their name. This shared allegiance is not, as Rousseau and others argued, a contract among the living. It is a partnership between the living, the unborn and the dead – a continuous trust that no generation can pillage for its own advantage.

It is with a great sigh of relief that I read those ideas, delicately expounded by Jesse Norman in his recent biography of Edmund Burke. For Norman is a rising star in parliament, and inspires the hope that the Tory party might be waking up to the need for a believable philosophy if it is not to lose its real following.

Our situation today mirrors that faced by Burke. Now, as then, abstract ideas and utopian schemes threaten to displace practical wisdom from the political process. Instead of the common law of England we have the abstract idea of human rights, slapped on us by European courts whose judges care nothing for our unique social fabric. Instead of our inherited freedoms we have laws forbidding 'hate speech' and discrimination that can be used to control what we say and what we do in ever more intrusive ways. The primary institutions of civil society – marriage and the family – have no clear endorsement from our new political class. Most importantly, our parliament has, without consulting the people, handed over sovereignty to Europe, thereby losing control of our borders and our collective assets, the welfare state included.

In its attempt to address the economic legacy of Labour's spendthrift policies and the widespread abuse of the welfare system the party has the full support of its traditional constituency. Nevertheless, it seems unaware that, in the hearts of conservative voters, social continuity and national identity take precedence over all other issues. Only now, when wave after wave of immigrants seek the benefit of our hard-won assets and freedoms, do the people fully grasp what loss of sovereignty means. And still the party hesitates to reverse the policies that brought us to this pass, while the old guard of Europeanists defend those policies in economic terms, seemingly unaware that the question is not about economics at all.

In other matters, too, it is not the economic cost that concerns the conservative voter but the nation and our attachment to it. Not understanding this, the government has embarked on a politically disastrous environmental programme. For two centuries the English countryside has been an icon of national identity and the loved reminder of our island home. Yet the government is bent on littering the hills with wind turbines and the valleys with high-speed railways. Conservative voters tend to believe that the 'climate change' agenda has been foisted on us by an unaccountable lobby of politicized intellectuals. But the government has yet to agree with them, and meanwhile is prepared to sacrifice the landscape if that helps to keep the lobbyists quiet.

Conservatives believe, with Burke, that the family is the core institution whereby societies reproduce themselves and pass moral knowledge to the young. The party has made a few passing nods in this direction, but its only coherent policy – sprung on the electorate without forewarning – is the introduction of gay marriage. Sure, there are arguments for and against this move. But for the ordinary voter the family is a place in which children are produced, socialized and protected. That is what the party should be saying, but does not say, since it is prepared to sacrifice the loyalty of its core constituents to the demands of a lobby that is unlikely to vote for it.

Many readers of the *Guardian* will not worry that the Tories are alienating their core voters. But they will be interested by Jesse Norman's take on Burke, since it shows exactly how, and by what kind of thinking, those voters might be reclaimed. And with Norman's recent appointment to the policy advisory board of the party, the opposition will have to take his thinking seriously.

What Trump Doesn't Get About Conservatism

(*New York Times*, 2018)

I have devoted a substantial part of my intellectual life to defining and defending conservatism, as a social philosophy and a political programme. Each time I think I have hit the nail on the head, the nail slips to one side and the hammer blow falls on my fingers.

Like many others, both conservative and liberal, I did not foresee the political career of Donald Trump, nor did I imagine that such a man could occupy the highest office of state, in the name of a party that specifically makes appeal to conservative voters. Is this simply an aberration, or are there some deep links that tie the president to the great tradition of thought that I describe in my recent book, *Conservatism: An Invitation to the Great Tradition*?

When describing the history of an idea, one naturally looks for its best expression. A history of liberalism will have a lot to say about John Locke and Jean-Jacques Rousseau, somewhat less to say about Hillary Clinton. A survey of the conservative idea will dwell at length on Edmund Burke and Thomas Jefferson and devote only a paragraph or two to Margaret Thatcher.

On the other hand, Mrs Thatcher, and to some extent Mrs Clinton, are known for invoking the great figures of political philosophy and for showing an educated awareness that 'ideas have consequences', as the American conservative Richard Weaver expressed the point. In Mr Trump we encounter a politician who uses social media to bypass the realm of ideas entirely, addressing the sentiments of his followers without a filter of educated argument and with only a marginal interest in what anyone with a mind may have said.

Americans are conscious of their constitutional rights and freedoms. These assets are not guaranteed by human nature and exist only because Americans have fought for them. And they have fought for them as a nation, facing the future together. National identity is the origin of the trust on which political order depends. Such trust does not exist in Libya or Syria. But it exists in America, and the country has no more precious asset than the mutual loyalty that enables the words 'we, the people' to resonate with every American, regardless of whether it is a liberal or a conservative who utters them.

Those first words of the United States Constitution do not refer to all people everywhere. They refer to the people who reside *here*, in this place and under this rule of law, and who are the guardians and beneficiaries of a shared political inheritance. Grasping that point is the first principle of conservatism.

Our political inheritance is not the property of humanity in general but of our country in particular. Unlike liberalism, with its philosophy of abstract human rights, conservatism is based not in a universal doctrine but in a particular tradition, and this point at least the president has grasped. Moreover, he has understood that the legal order of the United States is rooted in customs that the Constitution was designed to protect. In this, too, Mr Trump has shown himself to belong to the wider conservative tradition, seeking a Supreme Court that applies the Constitution, rather than one that constantly revises it, regardless of the elected legislature.

But, as Edmund Burke pointed out in one of the founding documents of modern conservatism, his *Reflections on the Revolution in France*, we must 'reform in order to conserve'. Institutions, traditions and allegiances survive by adapting, not by remaining forever in the condition in which a political leader might inherit them. Conservative thinkers have in general understood this. And the principle of adaptability applies not only to law but also to the economy on which all citizens depend.

In another of conservatism's founding documents, *The Wealth of Nations*, Adam Smith argued that trade barriers and protections offered to dying industries will not, in the long run, serve the interests of the people. On the contrary, they will lead to an ossified economy that will splinter in the face of competition. President Trump seems not to have grasped this point. His protectionist policies resemble those of post-war socialist governments in Europe, which insulated dysfunctional industries from competition and led not merely to economic stagnation but also to a kind of cultural pessimism that surely goes entirely against the American grain.

Conservative thinkers have on the whole praised the free market, but they do not think that market values are the only values there are. Their primary concern is with the aspects of society in which markets have little or no part to play: education, culture, religion, marriage and the family. Such spheres of social endeavour arise not through buying and selling but through cherishing what cannot be bought and sold: things like love, loyalty, art and knowledge, which are not means to an end but ends in themselves.

About such things it is fair to say that Mr Trump has at best only a distorted vision. He is a product of the cultural decline that is rapidly consigning our artistic and philosophical inheritance to oblivion. And perhaps the principal reason for doubting Mr Trump's conservative credentials is that, being a creation of social media, he has lost the sense that there is a civilization out there that stands above his deals and his tweets in a posture of disinterested judgement.

PART THREE

Why the Left Is Never Right

The Ideology of Human Rights

(*The Times Literary Supplement*, 1980)

Classical Marxism pledged itself to the abolition of the nation–state, and hid this pledge in a prediction. The local and historical allegiances that compose a nation, together with the constitutional devices that consolidate them, were described as 'superstructure', serving to protect and endorse a transient phase of economic development. As soon as nationhood 'fetters' economic development, then it must crumble away. The final resolution of history will be classless, placeless, timeless, international.

If the government of one nation can persuade the people of another to believe that doctrine, then it acquires superior power. It attracts attention away from local allegiances towards a cause that claims to transcend and replace them. The cause in question – 'international socialism' – is only an ideal, but it is also (it is supposed) an ineluctable reality, the outcome of impersonal forces which no one can resist with impunity or for long. The doctrine does not need to be proved; it can usually support itself negatively, by emphasizing the local grievances that generate the desire to believe in a timeless and placeless ideal. Its victims will rarely ask themselves what foreign interest chooses thus to beguile them. If there is an interest at work, it will seem to be their own.

It is fairly obvious that ever since Lenin converted the concept of imperialism to his uses, Russian foreign policy has advanced behind this internationalist doctrine. In most cases the advance has been to the detriment of that loose association of nations described, out of a Spenglerian sense of its destiny, as 'the West'. America, as the principal power among these nations, has perforce been their principal spokesman. But until recently American foreign policy lacked a convenient international doctrine behind which to conceal the pursuit of power. Striving for a nationhood of its own, America could hardly propose the removal of the nationhood of others a universal ambition. Under the Monroe doctrine American ideology licensed the interference in the affairs of other peoples only negatively: it was permitted to assist the attempts of any people to cast off the colonial oppression from which America itself was newly free. The aim of emancipating a nation from colonial power may often be right and sensible. But it is coherent only when the nation has acquired an existence apart from the power that colonized it. It would be absurd to assist the citizens of Shepherd's Bush in a struggle for 'liberation'. Shepherd's Bush does not, and never did, constitute a political entity, and has no consciousness of itself as such. Nor can it rise up from the midst of the United Kingdom and declare its historical right to self-government, or in any other way make show of its political self-consciousness as a fact to be reckoned with. Legitimacy is an elaborate artefact, requiring constitution, custom, usage and history.

The Monroe doctrine presupposes such a historical legitimacy to which to lend support against those who would usurp it. It must therefore prove an ineffectual screen for international policy towards peoples whose sense of their national identity is confused, fragmented or non-existent. What, such peoples may ask, are we being helped towards, when there is no identity which is naturally ours? The internationalist doctrine of Marxism provides a kind of answer, and it is one that hides, for a while, the interests of those who advance behind it.

Recently, Western foreign policy has had to be as ubiquitous as the foreign policy of Russia. It has therefore stood in need of a doctrine which is as positive and international as the predictions of Marxism, and also as immediate in its appeal. President Jimmy Carter, in identifying this doctrine as that of 'human rights', merely draws on a fundamental strand in all American political consciousness; it is therefore rare for his followers to inquire what the doctrine means. But it is pertinent to ask, since our destiny depends on it, whether this doctrine can at least conceal our interests from those against whom we need to advance them.

The doctrine that there are 'human' (which is to say 'universal') rights has its antecedents in medieval theories of natural law, according to which there are principles of justice which preside over the affairs of men independently of the local practices which have achieved the status of law. Authority is useless without power, but the Church gave enactment to the authority of natural law, by exerting international influence. Right and might did not diverge; moreover, each seemed to stem from a single divine origin, so that the first neither concealed nor distorted the second. The question of whose interest was advanced by the observance of natural law did arise, but it never led to the rejection of the doctrine. When sovereigns were able to break from Rome, it was because they had acquired national churches, and a common law which enshrined those principles of natural justice that had formally been the property of an international Church. Such sovereigns appeared to be constrained not by an external power but by the internal conditions of their legitimacy. And still the name 'natural law' was used to denote the authority that interceded between sovereign and subject.

The subsequent history of 'natural justice' and 'natural rights' is complex but familiar. What was once owed as an obligation to God came to be thought of as a generalized obligation to humanity. But 'humanity' names no sovereign power, only the hope that men might live without one. So the authority of these 'natural rights' is an unhappy one; when right lacks power to substantiate it, its allegiance will begin to slip away. In the end only brave men may stand by it, in a spirit of tragic self-sacrifice.

Nevertheless, it is from the conception of 'natural rights' that the current American internationalism gains its credentials. 'Human rights' are rights that belong to all people, whatever local arrangements should constrain them. In upholding such rights America tries to put its authority behind a doctrine that will capture the support of every citizen everywhere, and will not presuppose any particular economic order – such as capitalism – as its precondition. But because American power is hesitant, qualified by the same sense of justice that informs its ideology, the upholders of 'human rights' will lack international protection. It is impossible to arm them, to send troops to their rescue or to excite them to insurrection as the Marxist may reasonably do in the name of his international ideal. So the doctrine is of little practical avail against its rival.

It could also be doubted that the doctrine is coherent. Perhaps it is; perhaps it is not. I do not know. Bentham described it as 'nonsense on stilts', but the authority is perhaps not a very persuasive one. Sometimes, reflecting on all that was meant by the 'natural law' of the scholastics, and on the 'sense of justice' which seems so real in the breach and yet so indescribable in the observance, I think that there is truth in the doctrine. But then, if there are rights, there must also be obligations. Whose? Against whom are these rights being claimed? And what is being given in return for them? We find ourselves in the depth of philosophical controversy, trying to uphold that there are rights which ought to be granted to each citizen by every sovereign power, irrespective of history, constitution and local complexity, and (so it would seem) irrespective of any right which the sovereign power can claim in return. To know whether this doctrine is coherent, we should have to examine again the questions discussed so inconclusively by Locke, Rousseau and Hegel: we should have to embark on efforts of abstraction that have defied the capacities of the greatest philosophers, and must inevitably escape the understanding of the common citizen, be he as intelligent as they.

We should not be surprised to find, therefore, that 'human rights' tend to become a cause of action only in the minds of people who have the historical consciousness through which to understand their local meaning. In the absence of that consciousness, the doctrine is felt merely as a kind of generalized anti-authoritarianism, a licence to the individual to take no notice of obligations towards the state, and to ascribe legal legitimacy to almost any gesture of rebellion. The children of the Iranian middle classes who were sent to America for their education absorbed from the idea of 'human rights' only the ability to forswear allegiance to established power. The influence of their 'education' spread to their contemporaries at home and was easily incorporated into old habits of vengeance. Young Iranians, having learned how to disguise barbarity behind the Western dignity of 'student', proceeded to invade the 'natural rights' of the only American citizens weak enough to fall victim to them. And there is no arguing with them. Islamic law has always vested the exercise of criminal justice in the sovereign and so dispenses quite easily with a doctrine of what is 'natural' irrespective of place and time. It need make no room for the 'human rights' which, propagated by American liberalism, served merely to instruct the violators of right in the arts of injustice. Rebellion that has vengeance and not natural justice as its aim is a local affair, indifferent to the large metaphysical questions of the rights of man. The ideology of 'human rights' fails, and with it the foreign policy that sought to advance behind it.

The case should be compared with that of Eastern Europe, where traditional forms of law, surviving as custom, as memory and as reality in the Church's renewed temporal power, give support to the idea of an authority that mediates between citizen and sovereign. The doctrine of 'human rights' begins now to refer to something specific and cogent – not, indeed, to any universal ideal, but rather to old habits of allegiance and constitution towards which history has generated independent respect. The so-called 'dissident' in Czechoslovakia is no more universalist in his attachments than the Iranian zealot. He seeks to find, in the constitution of his country, a regard for that process of law to which his sense of historical identity directs him. If he speaks of 'human rights' it is because his loyalty is being required by an arrangement that promises certain privileges in return, privileges that can be understood in terms of the great tradition of European sovereignty. Such privileges are intimately bound up with complex local customs. They have indeed been overlaid and qualified by a Draconian law of sedition, and this law seems to be understood neither by those who enact nor by those who apply it. But the old privileges persist in the memory, being part of the sense of place, time and nationhood without which there could be no serious allegiance to the Czechoslovakian state. It is this historical content which makes 'human rights' intelligible, and so enables the citizen to feel instinctively when his rights are being denied. What suffers in that denial is not the citizen's 'natural' freedom (which would be nasty, brutish and short) but the more concrete, qualified freedom which is the condition of national identity. The cause of 'human rights', while it involves a clear appeal to justice, becomes a part of patriotism, inseparable from the love of tradition, language, custom and history that internationalism seeks to dissolve. But in that case, once again, the ideology of 'human rights' provides legitimacy to no ubiquitous foreign policy, becoming absorbed into loyalties that are immovably local and self-regarding. The nation survives as the principal object of affection and despair, and no new allegiance is formed to replace it.

Many of the places where foreign policy really matters are characterized by civil bonds that are both extremely local (scarcely deserving the name of nationhood) and extremely atavistic, having never transcribed themselves into constitution, sovereignty or law. It is hardly likely that the doctrine of 'natural rights', redolent as it is of Western constitutionalism and the traditions of Roman law, will provide the inspiration to people seeking to 'emerge' out of timelessness into history. But it is likely that Marxism, which speaks the language of might and not of right, will at least be understood by them. Paradoxically enough, it is by reaching towards that 'higher' form of timelessness promised by the Marxist that Africans often begin to envisage themselves as constrained by interests that are both local and also internationally recognized. In other words, this peculiar form of internationalism can catalyse a developing sense of nationhood.

We must not be surprised, then, if the nationalism of emergent peoples throws in its lot with Marxism and not with the doctrine of 'human rights'. Our power, having adopted an ideology that retards its exercise, seems fragile beside that of Russia. The Russians disguise foreign policy behind a theory that, however internationalist in its ultimate meaning, is understood by its victims as the sanction of a budding nationalism, and which hence becomes an object of all the allegiances that matter to them most.

Who is a Fascist?

(*The Times*, 1983)

Mr Tony Benn is not the only one to use the word 'fascist' as a term of abuse for those who are unconvinced by the theory of practice of socialism. Almost everyone on the right (to use another indiscriminate label) is liable to be faced by the following argument. You believe a, b and c. At least some fascists believed a, b and c. Ergo you are a fascist. Since fascism is evil, you too are evil. In Mrs Thatcher's case a, b and c are the ethic of work, the values of the family and national sovereignty. (*Travail, famille, patrie*, in the words of Vichy France.) They might have been love, life and happiness for all that the argument shows.

Such is the logic of Mr Benn. And it is a logic which has enormous appeal for those who have swallowed the myth that fascism is the enemy of modern civilization, and socialism (including communism) its friend. It is proof of the good manners of the right that it seldom replies in kind; but there comes a point where good manners have to be set aside.

Fascism was a system of government introduced into Italy by Mussolini. It has something in common with the falangism introduced by Franco into Spain; it also led to an alliance with Hitler. As a result, the term 'fascism' has come to denote three very different systems of government and is used as a term of abuse largely by those who regard it as a name for the mass hysteria which facilitated Hitler's crimes.

Hitler's regime in fact called itself 'national socialism'. It had very little in common with the regimes of Mussolini and Franco, other than the fact of massive popular support. This popular support has provoked the Communist Party – an elite organization generally incapable of persuading the mass of people spontaneously to follow it – into pouring vitriolic abuse on fascism in all its forms. But this should not blind us to the fact that the actual aims of Soviet communism have coincided very closely with those of Hitler: control from above; a command structure throughout the economy, and throughout civil life; absorption of all institutions into those of the state; destruction by whatever means, however unscrupulous, of all opposition; the control of thought, feeling, hope, fear and ambition through propaganda.

The difference between the two is fairly summarized in their names: one calls itself national socialism, the other international. Hence the first has been a little more selective in its choice of enemy. It is vitally necessary for this kind of regime to create a myth of the 'enemy'. For national socialism the enemy consisted in those within the state who did not belong to – and who 'therefore' secretly worked to destroy – the nation. For international socialism the enemy was a worldwide conspiracy, whose power base was the 'bourgeois' class: that is, everyone from capitalist to kulak. In each case the enemy enjoyed the same fate.

It is, I believe, extremely confusing to apply the term 'fascism' equally to national socialism and to the Mediterranean ideas of authoritative government espoused by Mussolini and Franco. Of course there are common features, and common dangers. But these should not be allowed to obscure the very real differences.

The essential feature of Mussolini's fascism was the corporation. The entire economic activity of the state was to be organized into corporations, subordinate to the state and answerable to it. These corporations would be composed of syndicates, representing the interests of workers, employers and professionals. Through the complex process of representation, all grievances would be removed and conflicts resolved within the corporation. Hence, if the syndicates – such as the trade unions and the associations of managers – performed their function, no other form of representation would be necessary. Government could be carried on by a small elite of dedicated professionals. Unlike national socialism, fascism did not set out to destroy autonomous institutions, but attempted to reconcile its belief in a command economy with a measure of free association at every level of society.

All very naïve, of course, but remarkably similar to the political philosophy of Mr Benn, and very different from anything that has been advocated or pursued by Mrs Thatcher. Unlike Mr Benn and the fascists, Mrs Thatcher has perceived that trade unions are not normally representative of the interests of their members, the representation cannot, in general, occur outside strong parliamentary institutions resistant to rapid constitutional change, and that the laws exist precisely to curtail the power of corporations, so that the individual grievance may be heard and the individual life find its purpose.

Fascism in Italy was doomed by the alliance with national socialism. In Spain a similar system of government escaped destruction and provided one of the more flexible forms of authoritarian control. Although imposed by military force, it was able to evolve to the point where parliamentary democracy could be initiated, along with the constitutional monarchy that provides such valuable support to it. We should take comfort from the example. It shows that, if Mr Benn's philosophy ever does gain wide acceptance, we might yet recover from its imposition.

Bennite fascism therefore holds out a promise that neither national nor international socialism has been able to fulfil. If we have to choose between these three evils, then no doubt we should vote for Mr Benn. Far better, however, to remain with Mrs Thatcher.

In Praise of Privilege

(*The Times*, 1983)

In the minds of many Labour politicians the principal social disorder is privilege, and a Labour victory, either now or in some future election, would certainly initiate a renewed persecution of those who are thought to possess this elusive quality. Hatred of privilege is, I believe, the true reason for the desire to abolish the House of Lords (Britain's most harmless institution) and for the hostility towards private schools and private medicine. What, then, is privilege, and why is it bad?

There are two kinds of privilege: one the product of freedom, the other the product of power. The first kind is a necessary consequence of association. Suppose John, William and Mary have a common interest in mountaineering. They form a club, so as to buy equipment and furnish expeditions. In due course William retires, bequeathing his equipment to the club; John and Mary invite other members. Naturally they consider only those who will be suitable companions. Hence conditions of membership soon emerge. The club is successful, buys itself rights and offers unique advantages to members. It continues, long after the death of John and Mary, a living memorial to their association. What was once a bond of mutual affection has become a body of rules, an institution, a system of privilege. Existing members will seek to limit the number of entrants and to secure advantages for their friends and children. Such little systems of privilege are the inevitable result of free association and can be prevented only by force.

The second kind of privilege is a consequence of command. An officer can command his troops only if he can call on a habit of obedience, established by some hierarchy of power. Such hierarchies exist wherever there is leadership and government, although they differ widely in the kind of sanction they exercise. They are necessary; but they are also resented, and will inevitably be resented unless subjected to a code of honour.

A person must command only that which is permitted by his office. Otherwise he abuses those beneath him. When the code of honour is scrupulously observed, we think of the officer as in a position not of privilege but of authority. If he abuses his office, for personal gain, then his power becomes a source of privilege. It is this kind of privilege which is most resented. For, unlike the first kind, it is inherently unjust.

The universal experience of 'actually existing socialism' – the socialism imposed wherever possible by the heirs of Lenin – is of the abolition of the first kind of privilege and its replacement by the second. The process – announced by Lenin as the 'withering away of the state' – might be better described as 'the withering away of society'. The misdirected zeal with which Leninism tore down every social institution was also applied to the building of the Communist Party – the most terrifying hierarchy of command that the world has ever known. Every office in this hierarchy presents opportunities for corruption, and the resulting system of privilege has a scale and scope that defy description. It is contemptuous of honour and hostile to freedom, especially to the freedom of association. It has abolished altogether those moral genial privileges that are the condition of civilized existence. Anyone who wishes to know what is hateful in privilege should therefore look at the socialist states.

The privileges denounced by the Labour Party belong largely to the first kind. They result not from a hierarchy of command but from a society rich in institutions, based in voluntary association, in charity and in the endeavour of creative individuals who have wished not to dominate but to unite with their fellows.

Consider the public schools. These were established by charitable men and women who wished to form societies dedicated to learning and religion. The resulting institutions are not, and were never intended to be, state institutions, and they have no coercive powers. Their members are chosen according to criteria that have evolved over centuries, through successive glosses on the original intentions of the founders, modified as ever by the natural human instinct to offer favours to friends. The ensuing privilege is spontaneous and irrepressible. Whatever happens to 'state' education, such schools will continue to provide education and also to produce lasting associations between those who have attended them.

A society that permits free association permits this kind of privilege. It is not obvious that such privilege is harmful, or even that it is widely resented. It is exclusive, but only in the way that families are exclusive: by including less than everyone. And people are more disposed to accept 'exclusiveness' now that they have seen what follows from its abolition. For it is evident that small voluntary institutions are better able to do what they propose to do than the substitutes offered (and usually controlled) by the state.

In order to curtail social privilege, therefore, we must curtail the freedom to associate. We must follow in Lenin's footsteps and erect a system of control that will be sufficient to abolish man's natural propensity towards institution-building. We then replace association by coercion, and the privileges of society by the far more threatening privileges of the state.

A Hominist Homily

(*The Times*, 1984)

There is no force more dynamic, more progressive, more avid for improvements than the force of human folly. Lest he should forget this, a teacher must repeatedly acquaint himself with books that he would rather eat than read. The other day, therefore, I shut myself away with a pile of feminist literature, and for some time my mind was numbed by what must be the most boring form of collective paranoia since Mussolini. Overcome at last, I fell into a deep stupor and began to dream.

I seemed to be in a London club, in a room heavy with tobacco smoke; all around me were smart City gentlemen. They had been drinking, and their voices rang out in a cheerful, boorish cacophony. One voice, however, thinner, higher, but more strident than the rest, made itself heard above the chorus. It belonged to a young man who wore a necklace in place of a tie and who was trying to win attention. Undeterred by the indifference of his neighbours, he raised his voice ever more loudly until, taking advantage of a lull, he jumped from his chair, waved his arms and commanded the room in the name of justice to be silent. With a murmur of acquiescence, his astonished companions sat back in their chairs.

'Men,' he cried, 'I address you as members of the largest oppressed class in the history of the world, victims of centuries of exploitation. The time has come to rise up against your oppressor. The time has come to rid yourself of your mistress, woman.' A few hands were raised in protest, but were at once turned towards the nearest glass of port.

'Look at yourselves: look at the devastation wrought in you by matriarchal society. Your work, your talents, your energies – all these are removed from you. For the sake of her and her children, your days must be sacrificed to humiliating toil. To provide her with home, comforts, pleasures, you must renounce all hope for a life of your own. By day you belong to your work; by night you belong to her, returning always in defeat from your little experiments in freedom to the prison that she has built from the product of your labour.

'Under matriarchal order, men are oppressed in their very psychology, subject to a jealousy more terrible than any force of arms. They must bend their projects, their actions and their thoughts in the direction imposed on them by woman. In every act they are subject to woman's morality, which scorns all tiny liberties and commands obedience to the law of home. Between the home where she commands you and the work towards which she compels you, only a few little crevices of freedom remain, and these too are threatened. Your lunches, your breaks, your business trips, all these are closely surveyed. In all your meetings and conversations you are exposed to her interruptions, her egoism and her domineering abuse. She has even pursued you to the door of your club, and now beats upon it, claiming rights of membership!' A mild protest arose, and the speaker leaned forward with an intenser stare. Strangely, however, the more intensely he stared at them, the less interest did his audience seem to show in what he said.

'Do not be deceived,' he continued. 'Do not think that our enslavement is merely external, a matter only of unjust institutions and unjust laws, which compel us to assume the burden of her maintenance. No, there is another slavery, an inward slavery, prepared for us in the most intimate encounter with our enemy, who withholds her favours until we offer the "commitment" which she demands.

'This is the most sinister dominion of all. We can obtain sexual solace only at the cost of liberty. Pleasure, for us, is also the supreme sacrifice. We are the means to satisfy her sexual craving – a craving so voracious as to demand a life of sexual servitude. For woman, man is nothing but a sex object, whose own modest needs are ruthlessly exterminated in obedience to her vaster imperatives.

'What is to be done? The answer, I believe, is clear. We must found a true hominist movement. Men must organize themselves as a class, to effect a change in the basic structure of human society. We must abolish the means whereby the matriarchal order ceaselessly reproduces itself. We must abolish motherhood. Let their babies be produced in test-tubes and brought up in battery farms. Let them work as we do, and suffer as we do the weight of others' dependence. Let every burden be shared.

'There must also be a cultural revolution, an overthrow of the illusions that govern us. We must fight the ideology of the family, the ideology of commitment and marriage, the ideology of female privilege and male subordination, the ideology that assigns all work to us, all leisure to our enemy …'

The audience was beginning to wilt. One gentleman had already slumped forward, his head resting on the table. Just as the speaker was beginning to announce the overthrow of the capitalist system in the final emancipation of mankind, however, the dozing gentleman suddenly started awake, and boomed out: 'Do you know – he reminds me of my mistress!'

At these words I too awoke, and returned to the page that had defeated me. Its tone and language, I discovered, had been borrowed by my dream.

In Loco Parentis

(*The Times*, 1985)

A short while ago I heard a weatherhen of liberal sentiment defend the view that teachers should not strike. Teachers, she argued, have the *right* to strike, but it is a right which they should not exercise, since in doing so they damage the innocents who have been placed in their charge. The same argument goes for nurses, doctors and members of similar professions who are obliged to stay at work for the sake of those whom the state, in its wisdom, has put in their trust. I do not know which is more objectionable: the view that there is a 'right' to strike or the view that those who have direct care of the state's dependants are under some special duty not to exercise that 'right'. But it seems to me that teachers and nurses are as entitled to strike as anyone else. The fact that they do not is testimony only to the conscience engendered by their professions.

A strike is a conspiracy to frustrate the aims of a contract and thereby to coerce one of the parties. It may sometimes be justifiable to strike; but how such a thing could be a *right* I do not know. Every right creates a binding obligation to respect it. If there is an obligation to respect the 'right to strike', then no contract of employment could be sincerely made, since neither side would be committed to its terms. The contract of employment, however, is the cornerstone of a free economy, and to set it aside so easily is to threaten every right that we actually enjoy. Only in a slave economy is there a *right* to strike, but it is the mark of a slave economy that strikes are made illegal.

Teachers may nevertheless be justified in striking, since no other course of action may secure a proper reward for their services. The state compels all children to go to school, even those who have no interest in attending. In such circumstances a teacher's job cannot be easy. Anybody who has stood in front of a class of children for six hours a day, five days a week, and endeavoured both to control them and to retain their interest, knows that this is demanding and disturbing work. In an ideal world the teacher would receive a salary commensurate with the other professions and a social status equal to theirs. In such a world, however, the teacher would not be a servant of the state. Nor would children be compelled, regardless of their interests, to attend his classes.

The sentimental liberal believes that teachers, like nurses, have a *special responsibility* to those in their charge. Why is this? Parents are compelled to educate their children, and for most people this means sending them to a state school. The illusion therefore arises that children are really the responsibility of the state. The teacher, being the servant of the state who exercises that responsibility, seems to bear the burden of it.

Individuals do indeed have dreadful responsibilities – towards their parents, their children and those who are sick and needy – and these responsibilities are difficult to discharge. The state therefore offers a service that relieves us of a burden. Thereafter arises the superstition that the *state* has the duty that the individual found so painful. Finally, because the state is too abstract a thing to bear the brunt of our resentment, the burden is transferred from the state to its agents: to the nurse or the teacher who, in fulfilling his contract, also performs the duty that is really ours. When the servant has had enough – when he too says that he can continue to carry this burden only if properly rewarded – he is told that he has a *special responsibility* to those in his charge. By the perverse logic of the welfare state, the teacher becomes a father to children who are not his own, and the nurse's charity becomes an indefeasible duty of care.

In truth, it seems to me, neither the teacher nor the nurse has a special responsibility. If two people bring a child into the world, then it is *their* duty to look after him. If the state provides him with an education, then the parents receive a privilege. However, when teachers withdraw their labour the privilege expires, and parents must bear the full burden of a responsibility which is in any case wholly and immovably theirs. If they have to give up work in order to look after their children, that is what they ought to do. If it is a *hard* thing to do, that is because life is hard. But those who have children must expect on occasion to pay for this most comforting of human afflictions.

If it is difficult for parents to feel this duty, it is also because the state itself has weakened it. By making education compulsory, the state has imposed an obligation that most parents could not discharge unaided; and by compelling parents to part with their children for most of the day, the state fosters the illusion that they have no real responsibility for their offspring.

Teachers have suffered a drop in social standing partly because they are now seen as compulsory child minders for a state which refuses to recognize the right of parents to bring up their children, and for parents who refuse to recognize that they have not only the right but also the duty to do so. Teachers have suffered most of all, therefore, from our changed attitude to children. Nobody really knows any longer who has the responsibility for these strangers who encumber the world with their helplessness. Children come to us already branded by the claims of the state, and we are tempted by the superstition that the state really does have the rights and duties that it so impertinently assumes towards them. We inwardly renounce the claim to our children's nurture, and since the state offers education, most people willingly accept the bribe. After all, it needs a lot of education to realize that education is not so very important.

To rectify this situation will be a long and difficult process. But the process could begin, provided teachers would strike for a year or more, and provided the rest of us would rebel against the law that compels us to place our children in their care.

McCarthy Was Right on the Red Menace

(*Los Angeles Times*, 1990)

Christmas is the season of good will, the time when enemies are forgiven and friends restored to favour. It is also a time of 'rehabilitation', in which the outcasts return to the fold, to be welcomed back into human society.

All over Eastern Europe the process of rehabilitation is gathering momentum: those who were wrongly imprisoned by the communists are being compensated; those who lost their property are recovering it; those who suffered for their opposition are blessed with influence and power. People who have been vilified for years as 'agents of imperialism', 'enemies of the people' and 'fascist conspirators' are crowned today with heroes' garlands, and hardly a soul in the former 'socialist countries' begrudges them their triumph.

Charity, however, begins at home. In the long, hard fight against communism we too acquired our victims, whose rehabilitation is now a matter of the greatest urgency. I think in particular of a great American patriot whose name has been a term of abuse to intellectuals of my generation on a level comparable to the names of Adolf Hitler and Josef Stalin: Senator Joseph McCarthy.

Time and again decent people have tried to describe what communism really is, and to warn against the methods used to advance it, only to be denounced for their 'McCarthyism'. Time and again the senator from Wisconsin has been invoked to silence those who have pointed to fellow-travellers in our universities and diplomatic services.

For a while there was no worse accusation in the intellectual world than that of anti-communism, and no meaner place in the academic hierarchy than that occupied by the critics of Soviet power. And those who suggested that there were organizations – the British Campaign for Nuclear Disarmament, for instance – that were dominated by communists and used to further their destructive designs would be laughed to scorn, and all but driven from the academy.

The fact is, however, that McCarthy was right. Maybe he went over the top; maybe it wasn't necessary to point the finger quite so rapidly or in quite so many directions. But the poor guy was exasperated; he had taken on the greatest criminal conspiracy the world has ever known, and was all but weaponless before the secrecy and deception whereby it worked its grim enchantment. Of course, we don't know the full extent of the damage inflicted by our communists and fellow-travellers. But we have a fairly good idea. For example, it was thanks to the penetration of British diplomatic services during the Second World War that Marshal Tito's partisans were adopted by Western governments as the rightful rulers of Yugoslavia, and that the brave Albanians who went to liberate their country were betrayed to the communists. It was the influence of communists and their friends – in diplomacy, in the academic world and in journalism – that led to the easy acceptance of the illegitimate governments of Eastern Europe after 1948, and which caused us to turn a blind eye to the sufferings of millions, so as to lick the boots of their masters.

I think of the work of such historians as E. H. Carr, Christopher Hill and Eric Hobsbawm, of philosophical apologists like Maurice Merleau-Ponty, Jean-Paul Sartre and Louis Althusser, of the Establishment Sovietologists, prepared to sacrifice truth itself for the sake of that precious visa and those 'privileged connections' with the Soviet apparatus, so necessary to a successful academic career.

I think of those notorious Cambridge intellectuals Harold (Kim) Philby, Guy Burgess, Donald Maclean and Anthony Blunt, whose single-minded commitment to a cause that their moral poverty prevented them from understanding contributed to the deaths of thousands and the enslavement of millions more. Was not Senator McCarthy right to warn against this kind of thing, and to castigate the moral corruption of a philosophy that places Utopian internationalism above the real and comprehensible loyalty to one's country and to the people who compose it?

The truth about communism has been apparent, to anyone who cared to know it, since 1917. It is a testimony to the degeneracy of our intellectual classes, which on the whole, with a few brave exceptions, have not cared to know it, preferring instead to vilify those 'anti-communists' and McCarthyites who had the impertinence to remind them. In all the dreadful story of Western weakness and gullibility, a few people stand out as prepared to sacrifice even their reputations, even the respect of their fellows, for the sake of unwelcome truths. And by no means the least of these was Senator Joseph McCarthy.

A Focus of Loyalty Higher than the State

(*Los Angeles Times*, 1991)

Why have liberals tolerated communists while execrating fascists and Nazis, whose behaviour is so similar? Why did Hannah Arendt, in *The Origins of Totalitarianism*, lay the whole blame on nineteenth-century nationalists, and why did she not notice Lenin, still less his mentor Karl Marx? Why did so many liberals tells us that the communism of the Soviet Union is not 'real communism' when the very suggestion that there might be a real fascism, or real Nazism, free from the moral taint of the historian variety, would be dismissed as a despicable whitewash?

The answer is that liberals and communists share their most cherished belief: the belief in human equality. Mankind, they suppose, is one and indivisible, with a collective identity that transcends the primitive divisions of race, tribe and clan. The supreme evil is the attempt by one group to claim dominion over another: and no crime is more offensive than 'racism', which divides humanity in its very essence. From such premises, communists and liberals have advanced to a common conclusion: that national divisions are suspect and that national sentiments have no place in politics.

Recent events in Eastern Europe have added an ironic twist to this idea. Far from regarding communists as their common enemy and striving to be rid of them for ever, the nations of Eastern Europe are blaming each other for the catastrophes of four decades. The Croatians blame the Serbs, the Slovaks blame the Czechs, while the Romanians – well, if the newspaper *Romana*

Mare is to be believed, Romania's desperate plight is caused by 'Hungarian terrorism', 'Jewish revanchism' and the 'Gypsy disease'. Visiting Romania last month, I was left in no doubt that the seeds of inter-ethnic violence have been effectively sown. The question is, by whom and for what purpose?

I was not surprised to learn that those who call most loudly for vigorous action against Jewish conspirators, Hungarian terrorists and Gypsy dogs were until 1989 prominent members of the Communist Party, enthusiastic advocates of 'proletarian internationalism' and champions of 'friendship between peoples'.

Even more instructive is the case of Slovakia. Czechoslovakia's President Václav Havel, being suspicious of nationalist sentiment, refused to appoint the heroic ex-dissident Ján Čarnogurský as prime minister of Slovakia, for fear that Čarnogurský might lead a national revival. Instead, Havel nominated Vladimir Mečiar, a little-known figure who had pushed his way to prominence during the revolution by loudly declaring his allegiance to federal and democratic principles.

Within months, Mečiar was using every device of demagoguery to set the Slovaks against the Czechs and to persuade the Slovaks that a version of national socialism is the true answer to their drastic problems. Nobody who knows Eastern Europe would be surprised to learn, however, that Mečiar was, until the 1989 revolution, a member and secret activist of the Communist Party, trained in Moscow by the KGB. Fortunately, the Slovak National Assembly saw the danger in time, deposed Mečiar and appointed Čarnogurský in his stead.

We must see these strange events in their historical context. All the natural forms of social life – institutions, churches, clubs and companies – were oppressed or abolished by the communists. Politics and law were replaced by mock substitutes, and culture was driven underground.

It is hardly surprising, therefore, that people cling to their national sentiments, because these were the only form of belonging that the communists could not extinguish.

The answer is not to make war on national sentiment, nor to scorn it with high-handed liberal disdain. The answer is to find a focus of loyalty that is higher than the nation. We must look for an institution that occupies a place in the heart of the ordinary citizen while remaining above and beyond the turmoil of politics, a court of appeal to which every faction, every ethnic group and every religious confession may address itself. Such, indeed, was the Imperial Crown. It was this that created peace in Central Europe, and it is the loss of it that precipitated 70 years of conflict on the Continent.

Alas, however, monarchs are also regarded with ridicule by liberals. Peace and stability can come again to Eastern Europe only when the superstitions of liberals have ceased to be effective in politics. I suspect therefore that mankind must pass through many more years of suffering before reaching the happy day when an emperor of Hungary is crowned again in Bratislava.

The Art of Taking Offence

(*Spectator*, 2018)

The emerging witch-hunt culture would be an object of half-amused contempt, were we still protected, as we were until recently, by the robust law of libel. It is still possible to laugh at the absurdity of it all if you sit at home, avoiding contact with ignorant and malicious people, and getting on with real life – the life beyond social media. Unfortunately, however, ignorant and malicious people have discovered a new weapon in their unremitting assault on the rest of us, which is the art of taking offence.

I was brought up to believe that you should never give offence if you can avoid it; the new culture tells us that you should always take offence if you can. There are now experts in the art of taking offence, indeed whole academic subjects, such as 'gender studies', devoted to it. You may not know in advance what the offence consists in – politely opening a door for a member of the opposite sex? Thinking of her sex as 'opposite'? Thinking in terms of 'sex' rather than 'gender'? Using the wrong pronoun? Who knows? We have encountered a new kind of predatory censorship, a desire to take offence that patrols the world for opportunities without knowing in advance what will best supply its venom. As with the puritans of the seventeenth century, the need to humiliate and to punish precedes any concrete sense of why.

I recall the extraordinary case of Boris Johnson and the burka. In the course of discussing the question of whether the full facial covering should be banned here, as elsewhere in Europe,

Johnson humorously remarked that a person in a burka has a striking resemblance to a letter box. He was right. A woman in a burka resembles a letter box much as a man in white tie resembles a penguin or a woman in feathers resembles a chicken.

It was obvious to anyone with a smattering of intellect that Johnson had no intention to give offence. However, there was political mileage in taking offence – so at once offence was taken. One ridiculous lord (a Cameron creation) told us that the party whip should be withdrawn from Boris; MPs and public figures fell over each other in the rush to display their shock and distress that our Muslim fellow citizens should have been so grievously offended; even the Prime Minister stepped in to reprimand her former Foreign Secretary. Virtue-signalling was the order of the day. A kind of hysterical fear swept away all the important considerations that Johnson was putting before his readers, so that everyone, friend and foe alike, ran for shelter. 'We are not guilty' was the collective cry of the time-servers and wimps that govern us.

In reaction to this madness I ask myself who it is, in the matter of the burka, that habitually gives offence, and who it is that strives not to take it. We live in a face-to-face society, in which strangers look each other in the eye, address each other directly and take responsibility for what they say. This custom is not just a fashion. It is deeply implanted in us by a thousand-year-old religious and legal tradition, by the Enlightenment conception of what citizenship means and by a literary and artistic culture that tells us that we are in everything duty-bound to see the other as on equal terms with the self. Being face to face with strangers is at the root of our political freedom.

I was brought up in that freedom. I cannot easily accept that people should appear in public ostentatiously concealing their face from me. The British believe that strangers deal openly with each other and are accountable for their looks and their words. It is natural for them to take offence at those who brazenly hide their face, while nevertheless claiming all the rights and privileges of citizenship. I certainly feel awkward in the presence of such people, and suspect that they are abusing the trust that we spontaneously extend to strangers. Nevertheless, it seems to me a singular virtue in the British that they strive not to take offence, when standing before a black letter box, wondering where their message should be posted.

No sensitive person, however ignorant he might be of the Muslim faith, would fail to take off his shoes when entering a mosque – not because he feared the reaction of the worshippers but because he knew that long-standing custom requires this, and that not to observe that custom is to show disrespect for a sacred space. Somehow we are supposed to forget that principle when it comes to long-standing customs of our own. For us too there are sacred spaces, and the public square is one of them: it is the space that belongs to others, not to you, and where you meet those others face to face. When we encounter those who refuse to accept this, we are supposed to think that the entitlement to take offence rests entirely with them, and the tendency to give offence entirely with us.

Is it not time to get this whole matter into perspective, and to recognize that we must live together on terms, that Muslims must learn to laugh at themselves as the rest of us do, and that the art of taking offence might be a profitable business to the experts but is a huge loss to everyone else?

PART FOUR

Intimations of Infinity

De Anima

(*The Times*, 1985)

A philosophical question is one that cannot be finally answered. Some philosophers therefore say that such questions cannot be asked, since a question without an answer is not a question. This *gran rifiuto* has a certain dignity, but that is all. There can be provisional answers even where no answer is final, and since everything that matters to us is provisional, why should not philosophy matter too? Our experience bears witness to our need for philosophical answers. In morality, in religion – and now, alas, in politics – the great metaphysical questions ceaselessly obtrude, begging for an immediate and provisional reply.

One such question – considered by Professor John Searle in last year's Reith lectures – is that of the soul (or 'mind', as the philistines describe it). Is the soul distinct from the body? If not, whence arises our sense of obligation, what justifies it and how should we behave? Every human life contains a tacit answer to those questions, and the advantage of religion is that its answer is loud and clear. For many people, however, a softly spoken and hesitant answer is all that is obtainable, and the voice that utters it is heard only occasionally, in the pauses of an over-busy life.

It would not be right to describe Professor Searle as a 'still, small voice'. On the contrary, there is something loud and bantering in his argument that we are categorically distinct from computers and possess capacities that no machine could have. There are two reasons for being dissatisfied with what he says. One is that he constantly seems to assume what he must prove

– namely, that a machine can play with signs, but only we can *understand* them.

The other is that his argument is severed from all moral consequence. Even if we are, as he says, distinct from every artificial intellect, why should this matter to us? Is this the sign that we are free, that our lives have purpose and value, that death has lost its sting? Or is it just a weird addition to the sum of human misery: that we are not only, like the rest of nature, purposeless, but also cursed with the capacity to know how purposeless we are?

Religions have often encouraged the belief in the soul as an entity wholly separable from the body that incarnates it, a principle of freedom and value, the ultimate residence of the self. In morality and in worship, according to this view, the soul becomes aware of its separateness from the flesh and is inspired by the distant vision of its eternal home.

Almost all modern philosophers doubt that such a thing could be literally true, and many of them also agree with St Thomas Aquinas that it is by no means necessary for a religious person to believe it. The soul is neither separate from the body nor truly separable, and the promise of eternity means not disembodied existence in an unending future but the emancipation from time.

Aristotle suggested that anger is a boiling of the blood, but cautioned us that the word 'is' here does not signify identity. Anger is a boiling of the blood in something like the way that a house is the bricks that compose it. Similarly, the relation of the soul to the body is like that of a house to its bricks. The soul is a principle of organization, which governs the flesh and endows it with a meaning. It is no more separable from the flesh than is the house from its bricks, even if the soul may survive the gradual replacement of every bodily part.

It is to the soul that we respond when we respond to another, not to the flesh, even though the soul is nothing but flesh. In responding we see a meaning that we can transcribe in words only with the greatest labour – that of poetry, which is also the labour of the liturgy.

We do not understand another person merely by dwelling on his bodily constitution, any more than we understand architecture by studying it as it would be studied by an engineer. The appeal of religion lies partly in its ability to transcribe the meaning of the human form in intelligible symbols. Religion aims to extract the moral consequences that our bodily form implies, but which it implies too discreetly and too hesitantly to present a real obstacle to crime.

If you think of the soul in that way, you can also understand what it is to lose it. You lose your soul when you cease to find the soul of others: when you see others eclipsed by their bodies, their meaning extinguished by the physical laws which propel them. An example is provided by obscenity. In obscenity the human body invades our perceptions, overwhelming us with its reality as a psychological contraption. Seeing the body thus, unilluminated by the individual self, we see it as barren, disgusting and disposable. If we take delight in that, we are already lost.

More subtle ways are available, however, whereby the sense of the soul's priority is lost. Perhaps the most important – and characteristically modern – of these is through the great scientistic illusion according to which the source of human life is hidden from us: in the unconscious, in the 'material conditions' of economic life, in our history, our instincts or our genes. Such an idea – associated with every pseudo-science of man, from Marx and Freud to sociobiology – severs us more effectively than any superstition from our purpose and fulfilment. For it fosters the master thought of crime: the attribution of my life and actions to something that is not myself, and for which I cannot answer.

A Matter of Life and Deathlessness

(*Daily Telegraph*, 2001)

The creation of ANDi, a rhesus monkey with an alien gene from a jellyfish, by a team of scientists in Oregon brings us one step nearer the *Brave New World* of Aldous Huxley, in which human beings themselves are manufactured according to requirements laid down by their benevolent rulers.

Interestingly enough, the only complaints so far registered against the production of a GM monkey have come from animal welfare campaigners. No one seems to have warned against the new possibilities for the abuse of human beings that are opened up by this unconscionable treatment of so near a relative. As was shown by Parliament's decision last month to permit research using cells from human embryos, little now remains of the old idea that life and its genesis are sacred things, to be meddled with at our peril. The piety and humility which it was once natural to feel before the fact of creation have given way to a cynical exploitation of life, whether animal or human, for the purposes of its present trustees.

Those engaged in producing the GM monkey have excused themselves in the same terms as those who carry out research using human embryos. Their experiments, they tell us, may lead to a cure for the diseases of old age, such as Alzheimer's. The idea that there might be something inherently wrong in what they are doing is inexpressible in any vocabulary that they recognize. It is perhaps unfair to draw the comparison with Dr Mengele of Auschwitz; but it is certainly true that the new breed of medical researchers proceeds as though any reference to moral absolutes, to the sanctity of life or to the spiritual cost of meddling in its sources, is merely a quaint survival of a discredited view of the human condition. As in so many areas, cost/benefit calculus has taken over from morality, and the real costs, because they fall on creatures unborn, are disregarded.

The Bible's warning against this kind of presumption was reworked in the late medieval legend of Faust, and given its most polished form by Goethe. Faust's pact with the Devil brings enormous present benefits, but they can be measured only in this-worldly terms, while the cost is other-worldly. Our modern scientists seem to have little conception of that great black silence which will supervene when our knowledge finally destroys us. But there is no doubt that we are moving in a direction that ought to alarm us, and that the legend of Faust is as relevant to us as it was to thinkers of the Enlightenment such as Goethe.

With the conquest of each disease there appears another, reserved for a yet later age. And to fight these new and unnatural diseases we pillage the life around us – not animal life only but also the life of the youngest and most helpless human beings, who are dismembered for our purposes and then flushed down the sink. I have the horrible vision of a future in which there are no young people any more, except those manufactured by the bionic geriatrics who control things, and who use all the resources of the Earth, including those that belong by rights to future generations, to outstay their welcome on a planet whose resources they devote entirely to themselves.

Physical ageing has been overcome: thanks to Viagra, the loveless old geezers of the future romp like teenagers, but with ever-decreasing passion. Senility and disease have been driven over the horizon out of sight, and – since the planet is now chock-a-block with permanent residents – normal forms of reproduction have been outlawed, as in Huxley's dystopian vision. Official approval is needed for the creation of new human beings; and most of them are produced as spare parts for the gerontocracy. The result is not a world of eternal youth but a world of permanent weariness: the triumph of the body and the loss of the soul. Such is now the tendency of medical research.

Only art can enable us to imagine the spiritual state of these future beings who do not age and who look on all surrounding life as no more than a means to their own survival. And it so happens that there is a great work of art which addresses this subject, and which tells us in music just what the spiritual price will be: Janáček's opera *The Makropulos Case*. The protagonist of this work, Emilia Marty, has survived for three centuries, thanks to an elixir that confers the outward vestiges of youth. She has lived well beyond her capacity to love, to fear, to hope or to enjoy any warm human emotion. Her life is transparently worthless. But it suddenly regains its worth at the final moment, when Emilia sees its futility and boldly chooses to die.

Emilia Marty took 300 years to recognize what was once known to everyone: that to value life we must accept our death. Medical research, of the kind that has led us to ANDi, defeats its real purpose: it prolongs life by negating life's value.

Dawkins Is Wrong about God

(*Spectator*, 2006)

Faced with the spectacle of the cruelties perpetrated in the name of faith, Voltaire famously cried '*Écrasez l'infâme!*' Scores of enlightened thinkers have followed him, declaring organized religion to be the enemy of mankind, the force that divides the believer from the infidel and thereby both excites and authorizes murder. Richard Dawkins, whose TV series *The Root of All Evil?* concludes next Monday, is the most influential living example of this tradition. And he has embellished it with a striking theory of his own – the theory of the religious 'meme'. A meme is a mental entity that colonizes the brains of people, much as a virus colonizes a cell. The meme exploits its host in order to reproduce itself, spreading from brain to brain like meningitis, and killing off the competing powers of rational argument. Like genes and species, memes are Darwinian individuals, whose success or failure depends on their ability to find the ecological niche that enables reproduction. Such is the nature of 'gerin oil', as Dawkins contemptuously describes religion.

This analogical extension of the theory of biological reproduction has a startling quality. It seems to explain the extraordinary survival power of nonsense, and the constant 'sleep of reason' that, in Goya's engraving, 'calls forth monsters'. Faced with a page of Derrida and knowing that this drivel is being read and reproduced in a thousand American campuses, I have often found myself tempted by the theory of the meme. The page in my hand is clearly the product of a diseased brain, and the disease is massively infectious: Derrida admitted as much when he referred to the 'deconstructive virus'.

All the same, I am not entirely persuaded by this extension by analogy of genetics. The theory that ideas have a disposition to propagate themselves by appropriating energy from the brains that harbour them recalls Molière's medical expert (*Le Malade imaginaire*) who explained the fact that opium induces sleep by referring to its *virtus dormitiva* (the ability to cause sleep). It only begins to look like an explanation when we read back into the alleged cause the distinguishing features of the effect, by imagining ideas as entities whose existence depends, as genes and species do, on reproduction.

Nevertheless, let us grant Dawkins his stab at a theory. We should still remember that not every dependent organism destroys its host. In addition to parasites there are symbionts and mutualists – invaders that either do not impede or positively amplify their host's reproductive chances. And which is religion? Why has religion survived, if it has conferred no benefit on its adepts? And what happens to societies that have been vaccinated against the infection – Soviet society, for instance, or Nazi Germany? Do they experience a gain in reproductive potential? Clearly, a lot more research is needed if we are to come down firmly on the side of mass vaccination rather than (my preferred option) lending support to the religion that seems most suited to temper our belligerent instincts, and which, in doing so, asks us to forgive those who trespass against us and humbly atone for our faults.

So there are bad memes and good memes. Consider mathematics. This propagates itself through human brains because it is true; people entirely without maths – who cannot count, subtract or multiply – don't have children, for the simple reason that they make fatal mistakes before they get there. Maths is a real mutualist. Of course the same is not true of bad maths; but bad maths doesn't survive, precisely because it destroys the brains in which it takes up residence.

Maybe religion is to this extent like maths: that its survival has something to do with its truth. Of course it is not the literal truth, or the whole truth. Indeed, the truth of a religion lies less in what is revealed in its doctrines than in what is concealed in its mysteries. Religions do not reveal their meaning directly because they cannot do so; their meaning has to be earned by worship and prayer, and by a life of quiet obedience. Nevertheless truths that are hidden are still truths; and maybe we can be guided by them only if they are hidden, just as we are guided by the sun only if we do not look at it. The direct encounter with religious truth would be like Semele's encounter with Zeus, a sudden conflagration.

To Dawkins that idea of a purely religious truth is hogwash. The mysteries of religion, he will say, exist in order to forbid all questioning, so giving religion the edge over science in the struggle for survival. In any case, why are there so many competitors among religions, if they are competing for the truth? Shouldn't the false ones have fallen by the wayside, like refuted theories in science? And how does religion improve the human spirit, when it seems to authorize the crimes now committed each day by Islamists, and which are in turn no more than a shadow of the crimes that were spread across Europe by the Thirty Years War?

Those are big questions, not to be solved by a TV programme, so here in outline are my answers. Religions survive and flourish because they are a call to membership – they provide customs, beliefs and rituals that unite the generations in a shared way of life, and implant the seeds of mutual respect. Like every form of social life, they are inflamed at the edges, where they compete for territory with other faiths. To blame religion for the wars conducted in its name, however, is like blaming love for the Trojan War. All human motives, even the most noble, will feed the flames of conflict when subsumed by the 'territorial imperative' – this too Darwin teaches us, and Dawkins surely must have noticed it. Take religion away, as the Nazis and the communists did, and you do nothing to suppress the pursuit of *Lebensraum*. You simply remove the principal source of mercy in the ordinary human heart and so make war pitiless; atheism found its proof at Stalingrad.

There is a tendency, fed by the sensationalism of television, to judge all human institutions by their behaviour in times of conflict. Religion, like patriotism, gets a bad press among those for whom war is the one human reality, the one occasion when the Other in all of us is noticeable. But the real test of a human institution is in peacetime. Peace is boring, quotidian and also rotten television. But you can learn about it from books. Those nurtured in the Christian faith know that Christianity's ability to maintain peace in the world around us reflects its gift of peace to the world within. In a Christian society there is no need for ASBOs, and in the world after religion those ASBOs will do no good – they are a last, desperate attempt to save us from the effects of godlessness, and the attempt is doomed.

Altruism and Selfishness

(*American Spectator*, 2007)

The first piece of moral advice that parents used to give their children was contained in the Golden Rule: do as you would be done by. Christian parents backed this up with the parable of the Good Samaritan, Jewish parents with the commandment to 'love thy neighbour as thyself', enlightened parents with their own version of the Categorical Imperative. It all seemed very simple. After all, what is morality about, if it is not about living with others? And how can you live with others if you don't treat them as equals?

Two powerful influences have disturbed that old equilibrium. The first is the gospel of selfishness, preached by Ayn Rand. Don't listen to that socialist claptrap, Rand told us. It is just a ploy of the parasitical, to curtail the freedom of the heroes and to seize their goods. Rand's fiery mixture of free market economics and Nietzschean defiance proved intoxicating to a generation struggling to come to terms with the New Deal and the growth of the welfare state. By announcing 'the virtue of selfishness', she reminded her readers that creation comes before distribution, and that creation needs a motive. And what motive will drive people to take the risks required by wealth creation, unless it be self-interest?

Amalgamating Adam Smith's 'invisible hand' with Nietzsche's condemnation of the 'slave morality', Rand gave to the would-be entrepreneurs of the mid-twentieth century the courage to say 'get off my back'. By being selfish, she argued, I enjoy my freedom and amplify my power – so creating at least one attractive person in the sea of second-raters. But I also provide work and reward to others, helping those around me to be selfish, and therefore successful, in their turn. By being altruistic I merely waste my energies on useless people; and when the state is altruistic in my name, seizing my goods and distributing them among its ever-growing ranks of dependants, then freedom, creativity and wealth are all at risk, and futility rules.

Rand was a terrific intellect, in every sense of the word 'terrific'. She fired her ideas like missiles into all the citadels of opinion, with vivid characters as their advocates and engaging dramas as their proof. Her novels and essays may not be the highest literature, but they grab the reader by the throat and defy him to say so. And when the still small voice speaks up at last, questioning whether it is exactly selfishness that is needed by a free economy or whether there are not other aspects to human life, other things to strive for, other sources of satisfaction than the satisfaction of *me*, the reply comes: of course, that's exactly what I am saying! When a father works to provide for his children; when a woman spends her money on a person she loves; even when a man lays down his life for his friend – all this is selfishness, doing what one *wants* to do, because one has the *motive* to do it, because that is *what the I requires*. The opposite of selfishness is not disinterested love but the kind of slave labour that the state demands, in order to be 'altruistic' with the surplus. An economy based on selfishness is one in which people also *give*; an altruistic economy is one in which they merely *steal*.

It is not surprising if, after a heavy dose of Rand, people end up unsure whether selfishness is a good thing or a bad thing, or exactly how you must behave in order to pursue it or avoid it. Things have been made worse by the biological theory of 'altruism', defined as an act whereby one organism benefits another at a cost to itself. On this definition the lioness that dies in defence of her cubs is altruistic. So too is the soldier ant marching by instinct against the fire encroaching on the ant-heap, or the bat distributing its booty around the nest. Geneticists have worried about how to reconcile 'altruism' with the theory of the selfish gene, but the rest of us ought to worry rather more about the use of this term to run so many disparate phenomena together. Is it really the case that the officer who throws himself onto a live grenade in defence of his men is obeying the same biological imperative as the soldier ant that marches to its death in the fire? And if so, is there anything really praiseworthy about the officer's action?

Taken together, the Randian encomium of selfishness and the biologist's debunking of altruism seem to undermine those old maxims by which our parents brought us up. The moral motive is made to look either mistaken or trivial: either something to avoid, since it impedes our creativity, or something unavoidable, since it is implanted in our genes, just as it is implanted in the genes of the bear, the buzzard and the beetle. The idea that the moral motive is something to be *acquired*, by learning the habit of self-sacrifice, seems to have no place in modern thinking, and it is not surprising, therefore, if the moral motive has so little place in modern life.

Not that our parents were entirely blameless in this matter. My own father was none too clear about the distinction between caring for others and caring for yourself. When I protested that I was doing my duty in walking the dog, and therefore could be excused from the washing up, he retorted, 'But you enjoy walking the dog; so that doesn't count!' Like many a person brought up in the grim routines of northern Protestantism, he believed that no action could be truly dutiful if you didn't approach it with gritted teeth, and that pleasure was a sign of selfishness. His socialist opinions came from the same source: not a desire for justice but a resentment of success. My father was one of those people – and British society is as full of them now as it was full of them then – who make Ayn Rand look plausible. And maybe it was because I early rebelled against his outlook that I have never been persuaded by Rand.

Is it not obvious, from Christ's description, that the Good Samaritan enjoyed helping the man who fell among thieves, that he went out of his way, from an abundance of good will and from the sheer pleasure of giving, to set the man on his feet? And is it not probable that the priest and the Levite felt no pleasure at all when they passed by on the other side, and maybe that they did so with a cringe of self-loathing? Learning to love your neighbour as yourself is learning to take pleasure in the things that please him, as a mother takes pleasure in the pleasures of her child. To call this 'selfishness' is to abuse the language. A selfish act is one directed at the self; an unselfish act is one directed at others. And the truly unselfish person is the one who *wants* to perform unselfish acts, who *takes pleasure* in giving and who *enjoys* the prospect of another's success. This is not, as Rand would have us believe, just another form of selfishness. It is an altogether higher motive, one in which the other has replaced the self as the object of concern.

Moreover, it is a motive of which animals know nothing. The ant and the bee may obey the genetic imperative that sends them to their death against the intruder, but they have no idea of doing this for the sake of the heap or the hive. Not even the lioness, who fights to the death for her cubs, has any knowledge that it is for *their* sake that she does this, or that she is making them a gift of her life. The little word 'sake' is one of those words – like 'the' and 'that' – to which a whole book of philosophy could be devoted. Indeed, whole books of philosophy *are* devoted to this word, since that is what moral philosophy is about – acting not just for a purpose but for the sake of something, be it honour, duty or another person. No animal has the concept expressed by this word, or the motive explained by it, and to describe animals as altruistic is to place an immovable obstacle in the way of understanding their behaviour.

Unlike the officer who throws himself on the grenade, the lioness defending her cubs is not tempted to save herself. She is obeying a species need that we admire because we share it, but which we also pass beyond into another state of mind of which the lioness knows nothing. To act for the sake of others, when temptation pulls in another direction, is to obey an imperative that goes beyond every species emotion. It is to make a gift of oneself, of one's interests and at the limit of one's life; and the words of the Gospel – that 'greater love hath no man than this, that he should lay down his life for his friend' – describe what is really at stake in the moral life, namely, self-sacrifice.

Europeans, who are snobbish about American culture, are also shamed by American altruism. Once they have made their fortune, Americans devote themselves to giving it away. They lavish gifts on their school, their church, their college or their hospital, taking an obvious pleasure in doing so. They also take pleasure in others' success – an emotion that seems to have vanished entirely from European society. Of course, Europeans are great preachers of altruism. But the more they preach, the less they give. For they do not regard others as their personal concern: it is the state, not the individual, that has assumed the duty of charity, and when things go wrong – as in the recent floods in England – it is the state that must step in to help.

The core idea of morality, the idea contained in that little word 'sake', is rapidly vanishing from the European consciousness. The public square is full of moralizing language about hunting, smoking, drinking and other forms of enjoyment. But when you ask for whose sake this or that is demanded, the answer is always: yourself. The old training in 'sakehood', which our parents regarded as the first step in moral education, simply does not occur. We should not be surprised, therefore, to discover that European cities are full of disoriented teenagers who think of the laws of morality as rules of long-term self-interest, and who seem unable to imagine what it would be to do something for any other sake than their own.

Memo to Hawking: There's Still Room for God

(*Wall Street Journal*, 2010)

How did the universe begin? Some think the question has no answer – that it lies beyond the limits of human reason. Others think the question has an answer, but that the answer depends not on reason but on faith. What almost no one believes is that there is a single, rational scientific theory that tells us how the universe emerged from the primeval nothingness. How could there be such a thing?

When Isaac Newton proposed his laws of gravity, he did so in a spirit of awe and reverence before the simplicity and beauty of the physical world. He did not doubt that so perfect a design implied a yet more perfect designer.

Immanuel Kant, who believed that Newton's laws of gravity are not merely true but necessarily true, argued that we humans lack the ability to comprehend the universe as a whole, and thus that we can never construct a valid argument for a designer. Our thinking can take us from one point to another along the chain of events. But it cannot take us to a point outside the chain, from which we can pose the question of an original cause. Indeed, the question of how the universe began does not make sense. The concept of cause applies to the objects of experience, linking past to future through universal laws. When we ask about the universe as a whole, we are attempting to go beyond possible experience into a realm where the concept of cause has no purchase, and where the writ of reason does not run.

All physicists since Kant have been influenced by this argument. Some admit the point, like Albert Einstein. Others, like Stephen

Hawking, express the point in a language of their own. But Mr Hawking now wishes to break with this consensus and to argue that science actually does have an answer to the question of origins. We can know how the universe was created, he suggests, since the laws of physics imply that there are limiting conditions, in which universes come into being by the operation of those very laws. There is no room for the creator, since there is no need for Him. The laws of physics do it all by themselves.

Mr Hawking, of course, dazzles us with his scientific discoveries. Einstein broke with the common-sense view of the world when he decided to treat time as a fourth dimension, on a par with the three dimensions of space. Mr Hawking gives us dimension upon dimension, assuming that because every continuum can be squeezed into the axioms of a geometry there is no limit to the number of dimensions in which we humans find ourselves suspended. Nor is there a limit to the number of universes, even though we happen to inhabit only one of them and the others may be for ever inaccessible to us.

The laws of physics are fast ceasing to be laws of the universe and are becoming laws of a 'multiverse' instead. By the time people absorb all of these shifts, they have little strength left to dissent from the view that 'the laws of gravity and quantum theory allow universes to appear spontaneously from nothing', or to question Mr Hawking's conclusion that therefore there is no need for God.

But what exactly has changed? Have we really moved on from the position that Kant presented? Have we really lifted ourselves outside of everything and everywhere, and achieved the view from nowhere that tells us how things began?

If Mr Hawking is right, the answer to the question 'What created the universe?' is 'The laws of physics'. But what created the laws of physics? How is it that these strange and powerful laws, and these laws alone, apply to the world?

There are those who will say that the question has no answer – that it lies at or beyond the limits of human thought. And there are those who will say that the question has an answer, but that it is answered not by reason but by faith. I say that perhaps, in the end, they are the same position. That is what Kant believed. You find out the limits of scientific understanding, he said. And beyond those limits lies the realm of morality, commitment and trust.

Kant, who destroyed all the systems of metaphysics and dug a grave for theology, was also a believer who, as he put it, 'attacked the claims of reason in order to make room for those of faith'. It seems to me that he was right.

Humans Hunger for the Sacred: Why Can't the New Atheists Understand That?

(*Spectator*, 2014)

Does the world have a purpose? The new atheists regard the question as absurd. Purposes emerge in the course of evolution, they tell us; to suppose that they could exist before any organism can gain a reproductive advantage from possessing them is to unlearn the lesson of Darwin. With the theory of evolution firmly established, therefore, there is no room in the scientific worldview for an original purpose, and therefore no room for God.

Today's evangelical atheists go further, and tell us that history has shown religion to be so toxic that we should do our best to extinguish it. Such writers describe the loss of religion as a moral gain – even though, for most ordinary believers, it looks like the loss of all that they most seriously value. But maybe the atheists have misunderstood their target.

The 'god of the philosophers' – serene, omniscient and outside space and time – has appeal to those who think in abstract terms. But ordinary people don't think in abstract terms. They don't see God as the answer to a cosmological question, since they don't have cosmological questions. But they do have the question of how to live, and in the effort to live with others they often stumble upon moments, places, relationships and experiences that have a numinous character – as though removed from this world and in some way casting judgement on it.

Hence there is another question, which seems to be much nearer to the heart of what we, in the Western world, are now going through: what is the sacred, and why do people cling to it? Sacred things, Émile Durkheim once wrote, are 'set aside and forbidden'. To touch them with profane hands is to wipe away their aura, so that they flutter to earth and die. To those who respect them, however, sacred things are the 'real presence' of the supernatural, illuminated by a light that shines from the edge of the world.

How do we understand this experience, and what does it tell us? It is tempting to look for an evolutionary explanation. After all, sacred things seem to include all those events that really matter to our genes – falling in love, marriage, childbirth, death. The sacred place is the place where vows are made and renewed, where suffering is embraced and accepted, and where the life of the tribe is endowed with an eternal significance. Humans with the benefit of this resource must surely withstand the storms of misfortune rather better than the plain-thinking individualists who compete with them. Look at the facts in the round and it seems likely that humans without a sense of the sacred would have died out long ago. For that same reason, the hope of the new atheists for a world without religion is probably as vain as the hope for a society without aggression or a world without death.

I prefer to put evolutionary explanations to one side, however, so as to consider not the benefit that sacredness confers on our genes but the transformation it effects in our perceptions. A person with a sense of the sacred can lead a consecrated life, which is to say a life that is received and offered as a gift. An intimation of this is contained in our relations with those who are dear to us. There is a treasure house of poetry devoted to the word 'you', and it records the human need to be absorbed by someone else, to see you as calling to me from beyond the sensory horizon. This experience is not accessible to scientific inquiry. It depends on concepts, such as freedom, responsibility and the self, that have no place in the language of science. The very idea of 'you' escapes the net of explanation.

Atheists dismiss that kind of argument. They tell us that the 'self' is an illusion, and that the human person is 'nothing but' the human animal, just as law is 'nothing but' relations of social power, sexual love 'nothing but' the procreative urge and the *Mona Lisa* 'nothing but' a spread of pigments on a canvas. Getting rid of what Mary Midgley calls 'nothing buttery' is, to my mind, the true goal of philosophy. And if we get rid of it when dealing with the small things – sex, pictures, people – we might get rid of it when dealing with the large things too: notably, when dealing with the world as a whole. And then we might conclude that it is just as absurd to say that the world is nothing but the order of nature, as physics describes it, as to say that the *Mona Lisa* is nothing but a smear of pigments. Drawing that conclusion is the first step towards understanding why and how we live in a world of sacred things.

Nothing brought this home to me more vividly than the experience of communism, in places where there was no other recourse against the surrounding inhumanity than the life of prayer. Communism made the scientific worldview into the foundation of social order: people were regarded as 'nothing but' the assembled mass of their instincts and needs. Its aim was to replace social life with a cold calculation for survival, so that people would live as competing atoms, in a condition of absolute enmity and distrust. Anything else would jeopardize the party's control. In such circumstances people lived in a world of secrets, where it was dangerous to reveal things, and where every secret that was peeled away from the other person revealed another secret beneath it.

Nevertheless the victims of communism tried to hold on to the things that were sacred to them, and which spoke to them of the free and responsible life. The family was sacred; so too was religion, whether Christian or Jewish. So too was the underground store of knowledge – the forbidden knowledge of the nation's history and its claim to their loyalty. Those were the things that people would not exchange or relinquish even when required by the party to betray them. They were the consecrated treasures, hidden below the desecrated cities, where they glowed more brightly in the dark. Thus there grew an underground world of freedom and truth, where it was no longer necessary, as Havel put it, 'to live within the lie'.

Recently I assembled some of my impressions of that world, and the result is *Notes from Underground*, a novel set in Czechoslovakia in the mid-1980s, which explores love between two young people who stumble over each other in the catacombs, and who, in the ambient twilight, find the meaning that the system had tried to wipe away. We live today in the glare of affluence, and cannot easily discern sacred things, which glow more clearly in darkness. But we need the sacred as much as the young people of my story. One way to understand this is to look back at that place where truth and trust were crimes and love a reckless departure from routine calculation. I can observe it now from a position of safety, and am glad that those times of fear have gone. But I also regret that they are fading from our collective memory and that their lesson has still to be learned.

PART FIVE

The End of Education

The Virtue of Irrelevance

(*The Times*, 1983)

The power of education is mysterious. It exerts itself through complicity and influence, rather than through coercion or control. Such power is more durable and more popular than force. Hence political movements tend to posture as the friends of education, whether or not their real purpose is to destroy or limit it.

The defenders of privilege argue for quality, and therefore standards; the defenders of equality argue for quantity, and therefore the destruction of standards. In their hearts, however, they are each suspicious of education, which, by making privilege accessible, both challenges those at the top and perpetuates the distinction between top and bottom. Each side aims secret blows at education. Some try to prevent it from spreading, while others try to destroy it altogether by spreading it too thin.

Recently, however, a more effective strategy has been discovered. This is to make all education 'relevant'. Traditionally a large part of learning was devoted to subjects that are wilfully 'irrelevant' – such as Latin, Greek, ancient history, higher mathematics, philosophy and literary criticism. The syllabus recommended by ancient thinkers consisted almost entirely of such subjects. And the ancient instinct was wise. The more irrelevant a subject, the more lasting is the benefit that is confers. Irrelevant subjects bring understanding of the human condition, by forcing the student to stand back from it. They also enhance the appetite for life, by providing material for thought and conversation.

This is the secret which civilization has guarded: that power and influence come through the acquisition of useless knowledge. The answer is, therefore, to destroy the effect of education by making it relevant. Replace pure by applied mathematics, logic by computer programming, architecture by engineering, history by sociology: the result will be a new generation of well-informed philistines, whose charmlessness will undo every advantage that their learning might otherwise have conferred.

Not surprisingly, the main objects of this attack have been the humanities. A person who knows only engineering or microbiology finds himself hampered by his knowledge, which casts little light on his experience and leads to no new communication with his fellow humans. A person with a classical or literary education, however, inhabits a transformed world and sees meaning where others see facts. He is equipped not just to change the world but to interpret it. Hence he will interpret it in his own favour and become master of his condition. The major task is to destroy the majestic irrelevance that confers this power.

Considerable ingenuity has been spent in inventing 'relevant' humanities. The problem has been to conserve the outward prestige of education, as an embodiment of the reasonable approach to life's problems, while persuading the uneducated that there is a learning addressed to interests that they already have. The answer has been found to lie in the word 'studies'. When added to a relevant-sounding prefix (such as 'media' or 'communications', 'black' or 'gay'), this word adjoins to even the most half-baked enthusiasm an air of superior knowledge. Not only are you right, it says, to be interested in the problems of the media, of blacks, of homosexuals: there is also a way of converting enthusiasm into expertise.

Consider the subject that has done more than any other to discredit humane education in American universities: 'women's studies'. How did this subject come into being? When nineteenth-century philanthropists confronted the industrial revolution, 'more education' was their cry – and when Arnold,

Ruskin, Shaftesbury and Gladstone repeated it, more education there was. Similarly, you might think, when twentieth-century philogynists campaign for 'women's studies', they are merely repeating the age-old folly of the English in seeking educational remedies for problems that are beyond intellectual control. In fact, however, the appeal of 'women's studies' is precisely in its power to undo the effects of education.

Not only is it relevant, addressing itself to social and political problems that the uneducated student will instantly recognize; it also cuts across established disciplines, adopting and discarding methods according to imperatives that have no academic rationale. It therefore ploughs like a tank through the enemy's lines, and carries a swarm of believing students behind it. Of course, no educated person is likely to take it seriously. For it is impossible to isolate the work of women from a tradition created largely by men; it is impossible to understand the social reality of womanhood without studying manhood; it is impossible to hold the jar of civilization to the light and expect the masculine and the feminine to separate like oil and water.

But that is precisely the point. The value of such a subject is precisely that it destroys education. It keeps the student's mind so narrowly focused on his random and transient political convictions that, when he ceases to be obsessed with them, he will lack the education through which to discover what to put in their place.

The Open University and the Closed Mind

(*The Times*, 1984)

Like many people whose radio is constantly tuned to Radio 3, I often listen to the Open University, usually while washing up. Having heard the last recital and the news, and quietly dreaming at the kitchen sink, I am suddenly disturbed by a flourish of trumpets, followed by bright, cheery voices inviting me to learn. For whatever reason, the subject tends to be sociology, which sounds, if I remember rightly, something like this:

Announcer: Hello. This is Unit Four of the foundation course in sociology, and our topic tonight is the exploitation of the worker in capitalist society. We begin with a brief discussion between our two course lecturers, Dave Spart and Chris Toad, who will be putting alternative points of view. Dave will begin.

Dave: Hello. Yes. Some people think that the exploitation of the worker in capitalist society is an economic phenomenon, due to the fact that the capitalist class *as a class* controls the means of production and so compels the workers *as a class* to work for less value than they produce. That's the view that I'd like to put before you.

Chris: And I'd like to put forward the opposite view, that the exploitation of the worker in capitalist society is not primarily economic but political, caused by the fact that the bourgeoisie *as a class* controls the power structures from which the workers *as a class* are excluded.

Announcer: You will find these two positions spelt out on page 15 of your commentary, where you will see that, while Dave's view is that of Marx, Chris's comes closer to Gramsci. Which of them is right? This will be your topic for the coming week. Dave, once again I'll ask you to speak first.

Dave: Given that the capitalist controls the means of production, what need does he have to control the political process as well? Why not allow a kind of illusion of influence to the workers, by giving them votes, if that serves to maintain capitalist relations of production? Basically, bourgeois democracy is just a functional mechanism. What matters is the economic base. The real social relations between people are forged at the economic level, and that's where the exploitation occurs. You see this in the relations between men and women; also in the relations between whites and blacks.

Chris: But sometimes the superstructure takes over. I mean, the functional mechanism of bourgeois democracy can become an instrument in the hands of the capitalist class, as in Britain today. By controlling the choice of parties, candidates, issues and outcomes, the capitalist class can *create* the situation where the worker has no choice but to accept exploitative social relations ...

I confess to finding such dialogue fascinating. By creating little disagreements, framed in a common language, and by incorporating into the language everything that is truly questionable, an aura of rational argument can be sustained almost indefinitely, even though not a single serious question is asked, nor a single serious thesis provided. Dave and Chris assume, as their common ground, all the major Marxist claims: that there are social classes, that 'capitalists' form such a class, as do 'workers', that the first exploit the second, that they do so as a class and so on. But why is it illuminating to describe a society as capitalist, and why should we think of ourselves primarily as members of a capitalist society rather than as citizens of a liberal democracy? To the listener who asked those questions, Dave and Chris would have nothing polite to say.

That, of course, is what is meant by bias and, in my limited experience, the Open University sociology course is certainly biased. But why all the fuss? What is the harm in a few young dons yapping away at each other in Marxese, while others listen to their radios, taking careful notes?

It should be remembered that the Open University is not a normal university. Most of its students are older people, some retired, who for one reason or another have missed out on education. Their minds are neither impressionable nor truly open, and often little besides self-esteem depends on whether they obtain a degree. Moreover, if they wish to know what they are in for they have only to turn on their radios and give it a try. It is possible that someone could listen to Dave and Chris and feel a genuine relief at discovering exactly what he always missed, and exactly what he should most enjoy studying.

Anyone who is foolish enough to embark on an Open University sociology course without first listening to it, or who, having embarked on it, decides that he cannot tolerate the bias, is probably heading for a failure. And the bright student who learns to write a perfect examination answer in Marxese gains a precious reward from his studies: he learns a language that isolates him totally from his fellows and encourages both himself and them to renounce all attempt at dialogue. In that way many fruitless quarrels are avoided and many consoling illusions preserved.

There, it seems to me, lies the strength of the Open University, which, unlike such closed shops as Oxford and Cambridge, makes it clear from the start what a student will sound like when he graduates. And if people wish to sound like Dave and Chris, good luck to them.

The End of Education

(*The Times*, 1985)

Higher education has a loud voice in the media, a strong arm in parliament and a free hand in the public purse. It is one of the most powerful vested interests in the modern state, and better able than most to give proof of its indispensability. Those who wish to clip the tree of learning, to prune its rotting branches or merely to question the general value of a growth whose shade seems so lethal to every rival interest are, to those who live from the fruit of the tree, the rudest of rude barbarians.

Not surprisingly, therefore, the government's green paper on the future of higher education has provoked sincere and vehement outrage. And even if it is less uncouth than most of its critics, the paper is undeniably deficient in tact and understanding. It argues, reasonably enough, that education should be funded by the public only if it benefits the public. But its utilitarian idea of benefit, suggesting that there might be an economic standard of academic success, is riddled with confusions.

Economics is, of course, a primary concern of responsible government. And the country can prosper only if it produces the right kind of 'human capital'. Hence polytechnics and universities have a vital economic function. Prosperity, however, is not an end but a means: it is the *sine qua non,* which guarantees nothing. We should not value education as a means to prosperity, but prosperity as a means to education. Only then will our priorities be right. For education, unlike prosperity, is an end in itself.

This is not to say that the government is wrong to consider the economics of higher education, or to seek a suitable return for the expenditure of public money. It must be clear, however, not only about its own priorities but also about the priorities of those whom it seeks to discipline. Academics value learning not for its economic results but for its own sake; they teach not to provide a pecuniary advantage but for its own sake; they do research not to stimulate the economy but for its own sake. Of course, education is also profitable. But if you fix your eye too firmly on the profit, you lose sight of the thing itself.

Education is like friendship: it brings help, comfort, strength, privilege and success. Friendship is unquestionably profitable. However, you must never value friendship for the profit that it brings. To treat friendship as a means is to lose the capacity for friendship. Your companion is no longer your friend when you begin to weigh him in the balance of advantage. So it is with education: the profit of education persists only so long as you don't pursue it.

Furthermore, the profit comes to us by an 'invisible hand'. Economic planning is no more likely to succeed in this field than in any other. Who could have foreseen that a society whose elite was educated primarily in languages that are no longer spoken should prove capable of managing the largest, the most profitable and the most powerful colonial administration that the world has known? And who could have foreseen that a society whose educational system is dedicated to science and technology should have produced only indifferent science, faulty technology and a flourishing underground culture profoundly hostile to both?

In this area wise planning means the careful avoidance of plans. Research must take its own course, guided only by that interest in truth without which it has neither result nor motive. And education should provide not the narrow details of tomorrow's technology (which will soon be yesterday's) but the intellectual discipline that adapts itself to new and changing circumstances precisely because it is attached to none. Higher education, in short, must be pointless and irrelevant. Otherwise it has no value.

That said, it is only fair to praise the government for questioning much that passes for higher education in this country. When the tide of drivel has swollen to such proportions that the University of Bradford can offer a first degree in a subject ('peace studies') that doesn't even exist, it is surely time to ask whether there might not be better uses for the taxpayer's money.

Take an impartial look at a modern campus, at the literature that students are asked to study, the questions they are required to answer, the standards of conduct to which they are expected to conform, and ask yourself how far what you observe accords with any ideal of disinterested learning. Or attend a conference of the British Sociological Association and listen to semi-literate papers defending 'the social construction of solidarity in the face of a dual strategy of paternalism and repression', the thesis that 'women are policed through the control of their bodies' and the idea that 'flashing' is an instrument of male domination. Or pick up a copy of one of the new journals of literary theory, *Semiotica*, for instance, or *Poetics Today*, and wade through the acres of jargon produced by people who can neither write with skill nor read with understanding, and who have lost all sense of the difference between a genuine question and a will-o'-the-wisp.

Perform any of those exercises and then ask yourself whether the expansion of higher education has really produced, on the whole, the disciplined intellect and cultured perception that the critics of the green paper suppose to be threatened by the government's parsimony. Ask yourself what has been the consequence of filling universities and polytechnics with academics who would not have been considered a generation earlier and yet who at once obtained tenure. Ask yourself whether bad education is really better than no education at all, and whether a government is really under an obligation to maintain the flood of vociferating ignorance that pours from our academic institutions. You will then perhaps commend the green paper for seeking to judge those institutions by *some* standard, even if the standard chosen is one that does not apply.

The Plague of Sociology

(*The Times*, 1985)

Auguste Comte, the father of sociology, was a naive and shallow thinker. But he had a concern for truth and a nose for problems. Under his tutelage sociology did not remain an academic dream but established itself as a science. Comte was followed by four great men – Marx, Durkheim, Pareto and Weber – each of whom provided concepts and observations indispensable to a full understanding of the modern condition. Furthermore, at the fertile interface of sociology and philosophy arguments and ideas have flourished which touch on the deepest and most enduring concerns of humanity. Pope John Paul II, for example, owes many of his moral ideas to such sociologically minded philosophers as Max Scheler.

Why then does sociology have the reputation that it has acquired? Why is it so often regarded as ideology, indoctrination and pseudo-science? Why does the mere mention of academic sociology serve to conjure images of an ignorant rabble lost in jargon, fired by doctrine and profoundly hostile to all forms of authority and power?

It seems to me that the image is not wholly unjust. Recently several academic sociologists, speaking at the British Association for the Advancement of Science, staged what amounted to a show trial of the 'New Right', denouncing their colleagues who had departed from the fold of socialism as morally corrupted and intellectually void. Not one of those colleagues was invited to reply, and the authority of the British Association was used as a badge of office with which to consign to silence all those whose opinions offended the bigots.

Academics who in this way silence discussion and who adopt a political stance as both unquestionable and the foregone conclusion of their subject are the enemies of scholarship. When the resources of a discipline are diverted to the task of fortifying a political dogma and protecting its intellectual weaknesses behind an impenetrable barrier of abstraction, and when those who question the dogma are dismissed as intellectually worthless and morally corrupt, we might justly suspect that we no longer have to do with an impartial science.

Consider the charge 'racist', so popular among members of the sociological establishment and now used to discredit the 'New Right'. The charge could be applied, on the grounds usually offered, equally to Marx, Pareto, Durkheim and Weber, and even to Comte himself. This is one small but significant instance of the way in which sociology has broken free from the intellectual discipline that created it and launched itself, a hysterical and overburdened boatload, on the sea of pure opinion – with nothing to guide it but its conviction that wherever it drifts is the right, or rather the left, direction.

Perhaps the most lamentable effect of second-rate sociology is its undermining of the natural language of moral intercourse. For bad sociology has only one intellectual device: the proliferation of spurious equivalences. Consider the favourite trick of the 'peace educators' – the representation of all power, however legitimate, however much the outcome of consent and compromise, as a form of 'structural violence'. (The trick was perfected by Mussolini's mentor, Georges Sorel, who himself took it by a devious route from Marx.)

Every social order requires a structure of authority and law whereby people are permitted to do some things and prevented from doing others. Hence every order, we are told, is founded on violence. Moreover, since those prevented and those permitted belong to different classes, every system involves 'structural violence' whereby the dominant class 'polices' the remainder. Against violence, violence is a legitimate response, and against the vast accumulation of 'structural violence' in the modern state any extreme becomes permissible – even terrorist violence.

Look at any course of 'peace studies' and you will find this nonsense purveyed as though it were a matter of dispassionate science. By the same argument, the power of the beloved over the lover, of the conductor over the orchestra, of the man who gives over the man who depends on his charity – all these legitimate relations become forms of 'structural violence'. However absurd the conclusion, we should not ignore the effect of the sociologist's language on the semi-educated. If you consider the change in modern attitudes to terrorism, in particular the changes displayed by the language of journalism, you will begin to see the extent of intellectual corruption. The terrorist gains legitimacy as soon as we are encouraged to condemn the 'system' against which he is fighting in the same terms that we condemn his deed.

'Peace education', child of sociology's most polluted slums, depends entirely on such spurious equivalences for its persuasive power. Totalitarian and democratic systems are represented as equal and opposite contenders in the game of nuclear defence, each reacting to an equivalent 'threat' presented by the other. Single-party government acting by conspiracy to suppress all rival sources of power is 'equivalent to the class oppression' of Western democracy. The rule of law is 'equivalent' to a tyranny of judges. And so on.

The use of these devices by town hall fanatics and street revolutionaries is to be expected. But their repeated occurrence in the academic discipline that dominates the polytechnics and universities of Britain is the sign of an appalling intellectual coarseness. I do not suggest that the founders of sociology are entirely blameless for the present corruption. On the contrary, impatient as they were for 'deep' conclusions, they too missed the fine distinctions and painted in the same grey colours the machinations of the wicked and the actions of the good. But even in their most impetuous moments they did not mutilate the common language of morality – our best reminder that in human affairs it is the fine distinctions which matter, and upon which our happiness depends.

Know Your Place

(*Spectator*, 2004)

The recent memo purloined from Prince Charles made the accurate observation that 'child-centred' education, by encouraging false expectations and discouraging effort, seriously hampers the one who receives it. University teachers know this, since they have to deal with the products of an education that puts self-esteem before real achievement. Despite the plethora of As and Bs gained through dumbed-down examinations in dumbed-down subjects, young people tend to enter university without the skills required for real study. The likelihood that an incoming undergraduate can read a book or write an essay diminishes from year to year, and only the entrenched sentimentality of the educational establishment prevents it from acknowledging that the cause of this lies in the culture of self-esteem. The ruling principle of our educational system seems to be that children should be made to feel good about themselves. The curriculum should therefore be 'relevant' to their interests, and examinations should make no judgement of their linguistic or literary skills.

Education is possible only if we persuade children that there are things worth knowing that they don't already know. This may make them feel bad about themselves, but feeling bad now is the price of feeling good later. The culture of self-esteem has the opposite effect: by making children feel good now, it makes them feel bad later – so bad indeed that they blame everybody else for their failure, and join the growing queue of resentful litigants. Education involves transmitting knowledge and skills, not illusions, and a practice devoted to persuading children that they are fine just as they are does not deserve the name of education. The acquisition of knowledge requires both aptitude and work, a truth so obvious that only decades of egalitarian propaganda could have induced so many people to deny it.

The fracas over the Prince's memo touches on deeper matters, however. Education is an end in itself. But it is also a means to social advancement. And there can be social advancement only where there is social hierarchy. In a society of equals there is neither failure nor success, and despair is conquered by the loss of hope. Real societies are not like that: they are shaped by competition, conflict, friendship and love, all of them forces that have distinction rather than equality as their natural outcome, and all of them profoundly antipathetic to the culture of self-esteem.

A society of real human beings is quite unlike the society for which children are prepared by a 'child-centred' education. It is one in which you can lose or gain, in which talent, skill and hard work are rewarded and arrogance and ignorance deplored. Social hierarchy is the inevitable consequence of this: not necessarily the static hierarchy of inherited social class, nor the hierarchy of property that tends to replace it, but a hierarchy all the same, in which influence, affection and power are unequally distributed.

Those elementary truths used to be acknowledged by our education system. When I was awarded a place at our local grammar school, my father, a socialist who jealously guarded his working-class identity, foresaw with a curse that I would 'get above my station'. And he was right, thank God. Both my father's resentment and my own success testify to the same underlying reality: that you can rise to a higher station in society by getting a good education. Thanks to my grammar school I gained a scholarship to Cambridge, and thanks to Cambridge I gained the kind of education that opened my thoughts, skills and ambitions to a world that I had never dreamed could be mine. And all this without costing my family a penny.

As a result of the culture of self-esteem, however, the helping hand that I received from the state has been withdrawn by the state. Grammar schools have been largely abolished, the curriculum has been vandalized (and also compelled) and the subjects that contain worthwhile knowledge – maths, the hard sciences, Latin, Greek and ancient history – have been driven to the margins of the system. And, having destroyed the schools, the state would now like to destroy the universities, by forcing them to take the dumbed-down products of its vandalism. All this shows a deep hostility to social hierarchy. But egalitarian dogma does nothing to abolish social hierarchy: it simply ensures that children at the bottom are given no chance to rise to the top. The way to make hierarchy acceptable is not to pretend that it can be abolished but to provide poorer children with the means to rise in it. In other words, it is to replace aristocracy and plutocracy with meritocracy. And that means doing the kind of thing that was done by my grammar school, and which is done by the Prince through his admirable Trust, namely, to provide young people with the opportunity to develop their talents and to reap the full reward for their work.

Now there are hierarchies only if there are people at the bottom of them. The advocates of self-esteem are so exercised by this fact that they try to invert the social spectrum, to represent the bottom as the top and the top as the bottom. Slovenly speech is praised as socially authentic, and ignorance as 'difference'. All forms of knowledge that require aptitude or work, or which aspire to a higher culture than that of the street, are dismissed as 'elitist' and driven to the edge of the curriculum. The music mistress who wishes to help her class to understand sonata form and its role in the classical symphony will be criticized for the 'irrelevance' of her lessons, which ought instead to be concentrating on the kind of music that young people prefer – Oasis, for instance. The suggestion that we ought to be teaching young people to prefer something better will be dismissed as arrogant and oppressive. This anti-elitism has the reverse effect of that intended, since it confines young people to the social position from which they start. But it has shaped the national curriculum in all the subjects that were once devoted to perpetuating our culture, and which are now devoted to flattering the child.

In an essay written over a century ago the philosopher F. H. Bradley reflected on 'my station and its duties', and said that the human being becomes what he truly is only by realizing his freedom in society, and each act of self-realization involves creating and adopting a social station. Whether you are rich or poor, smooth or rough, leisured or banausic, you become what you are through the circles of influence and affection that distinguish you. Unhappiness comes from being discontented with your station, while lacking the means to change it. And for all of us there comes a point when we settle in a social position that we have neither the power nor the will to change. It is from this sense of our social station that our duties emerge, Bradley argues. There is no single set of obligations, no 'duty for duty's sake', that applies to all mankind. Each of us is encumbered by the duties of his station, and happiness comes through fulfilling them. However humble your position, it comes to you marked with the distinction between right and wrong – a right way of occupying your station and a wrong way. Your duties may take the form of a professional ethic, of a specific role like that of doctor or teacher, of an office like that of prime minister. They might even take the onerous hereditary form of those imposed on Prince Charles as the Prince of Wales – duties that he takes extremely seriously.

If Bradley is right, then it is through the idea of duty that we come to feel content with our lot. The culture of self-esteem wants everybody to feel OK about themselves, regardless of merit. True self-esteem, however, comes through the sense of being right with others and deserving their esteem, which in turn depends on fulfilling the duties of your station. The office cleaner who conscientiously does her job is rewarded with the friendship of the workers whom she benefits. It does not matter that her social position is a humble one; for by occupying it rightly she earns a place in society as honourable as any other.

This is what George Herbert had in mind in those lines made famous by the Victorian hymn:

> A servant with this clause
> Makes drudgery divine:
> Who sweeps a room as for Thy laws
> Makes that and th' action fine.

It follows that a society can be hierarchically ordered without being oppressive. For every station has its duties, the performance of which is both an end in itself and a passport to social affection. And through education, ambition and hard work you can change your station, to arrive at the place that matches your achievements and which, through performing its duties, you possess as your own.

Universities' War against the Truth

(*Spectator Life*, 2016)

Young people today are very reluctant to assume that anything is certain, and this reluctance is revealed in their language. In any matter where there might be disagreement, they will put a question mark at the end of the sentence. And to reinforce the posture of neutrality they will insert words that function as disclaimers, among which the favourite is 'like'. You might be adamant that the Earth is spherical, but they will suggest instead that the Earth is, 'like, spherical?'

Whence came this ubiquitous hesitation? As I understand the matter, it has much to do with the new ideology of non-discrimination. Modern education aims to be 'inclusive', and that means not sounding too certain about anything in case you make people who don't share your beliefs feel uncomfortable. Indeed, even calling them 'beliefs' is slightly suspect. The correct word is 'opinions'. If you try to express your certainties in a classroom today, you are apt to be looked at askance, not because you are wrong but because of the strangeness of being certain about anything and the even greater strangeness of wanting to impart your certainties to others. The person with certainties is the excluder, the one who disrespects the right we all have to form our own 'opinions' about what matters.

However, as soon as inclusiveness itself is questioned, freedom is cast aside. Students seem to be as prepared as they ever were to demand that 'no platform' be given to people who speak or think in the wrong way. Speaking or thinking in the wrong way does not mean disagreeing with the beliefs of the students – for they have no beliefs. It means thinking as though there really is something to think – as though there really is a truth that we are trying to reach, and that it is right, having reached it, to speak with certainty. What we might have taken to be open-mindedness turns out to be no-mindedness: the absence of beliefs, and a negative reaction to all those who have them. The greatest sin is a refusal to end each sentence with a question mark.

As with so many changes in our language and culture in the past 25 years, the aim is to discover, and also to forbid, the hidden forms of discrimination. Almost every belief system that in the past seemed objective and important is now dismissed as an '-ism' or a 'phobia', so that those who stand by it are made to look like ideological fanatics.

In the 1970s, when feminism began to make inroads into the public culture, the question arose of whether there were not, after all, radical distinctions between the sexes that explained why men were successful in some spheres and women in others. Feminists rebelled against that idea. As a result, they invented 'gender', which is not a biological category but a way of describing malleable and culturally changeable characteristics. You cannot choose your sex, perhaps. But you can choose your gender. And that was what women were doing – redefining femininity so as to lay claim to the territory formerly monopolized by men. Thereafter, biology was removed from the picture and gender put in its place.

So successful was this strategy that 'gender' has now replaced 'sex' in all official documents and the suggestion that sexual differences are fixed has been relegated to the class of forbidden thoughts. Since gender is a social construct, people must be free to choose their own and anyone who implies the opposite is a bully and a fanatic. Even a pioneering feminist like Germaine Greer is forbidden to speak on campus lest her belief in real and objective sexual differences should threaten vulnerable students who have yet to decide which gender they are. Sexual difference has been marked as a danger area, about which beliefs, even those of Germaine Greer, are unsafe.

Just where this will end is anyone's guess. You thought that humans are distinct from other animals? Then you are guilty of 'speciesism'. You thought that there is a real and objective distinction between men and women? 'Transphobia.' You thought that attitudes which lead to mass murder are suspect? 'Islamophobia.' The one sure thing about the world in which we live is that if you believe that there are real and objective distinctions between people, you had better keep quiet about it, especially if it is true.

PART SIX

Fraudulent Philosophy

A Note on Foucault

(*Spectator*, 1971)

In the earlier work, now reissued, *Madness and Civilization*, Michel Foucault attempts to describe the place that civilization, since the Renaissance, has offered to madness. He traces the confinement of madmen to its origins in the seventeenth century, associating this confinement with the ethic of work and the rise of the middle classes. Foucault thinks that, as an historian, he should be concerned not with the origins of events but with their deeper significance. He reduces every object of historical study to an epi-phenomenon – a by-product and manifestation of what he calls the 'experience' that compels it. Thus he says, not that the economic reorganization of urban society *brought about* confinement, but that 'it was in a certain experience of labour that the indissolubly economic and moral demand for confinement was formulated.'

The madman is 'other' in the classical age because he points to the limits of the prevailing ethic, and alienates himself from its demands. But through confinement madness is subjected to the rule of reason: the madman now lives under the jurisdiction of those who are sane, confined by their laws and instructed by their sense of what is right. The resource of reason in this close encounter is to reveal to madness its own 'truth'. To lack reason is, for classical thought, to become an animal. The madman must therefore be made to enact the part of an animal; he is used as a beast of burden, and by this confrontation with his own 'truth' is finally made whole. Each successive age finds a similar 'truth' through which the experience of madness can be transcended into sanity. But Foucault suggests that the stock of these truths is now exhausted. The book ends with a Satanistic encomium of madness, in which Foucault appeals to the gods of the modern French Olympus – Goya, de Sade, Hölderlin, Nerval, Van Gogh, Artaud and Nietzsche – to testify to this exhaustion. Banal as it is, this encomium gains no substance from the studies that precede it.

It was clear to the eighteenth century, according to Foucault, that while madness was able to express itself, it had no language in which to do so besides that which reason could provide. The only phenomenology of madness lies in sanity. Surely then, the eighteenth century had at least one sound intuition about the nature of unreason? The province of language and the province of reason are co-extensive, and if madness contains its own 'truths', as Foucault claims, these are essentially inexpressible. How then can we rightly imagine a 'language' of unreason, a language in which the truths of madness are expressed and to which we must now attune our ears? The idea of such a language is the idea of an endless delirious monologue, which neither the man of reason nor the madman himself can understand. Such a language, even if it could exist, would bear no resemblance to the remorseless logic of *The Twilight of the Idols* or to the precise symbolism of *Les Chimères*. Foucault's heroes would have been unable to use this language, even in their final madness, and if we can understand them it is without its aid.

For the nineteenth century, according to Foucault, the experience of 'unreason' characteristic of the classical period becomes dissociated: madness is confined within a moral intuition, and the fantasy of an unceasing monologue of madness, in the language inaccessible to reason, is forgotten. This idea is to be resuscitated, however, at the beginning of the twentieth century, in the Freudian theory of unconscious thought processes that determine the behaviour of the irrational man. In the nineteenth century madness has become a threat to the whole structure of bourgeois life, and the madman, while superficially innocent, is profoundly guilty in his failure to submit to familiar norms.

The greatest offence of madness is against the 'bourgeois family', as Foucault calls it, and it is the 'experience' of this family that dictates the paternalistic structure of the asylums. The ethos of judgement and reprobation in the asylum leads to a new attitude to madness – madness is at last *observed*. It is no longer thought that the madman has anything to *say*: he is an anomaly in the world of action, responsible only for his visible behaviour.

In the asylum the man of reason is presented as an adult, and madness as an incessant attack against the Father. The madman must be brought to recognize his error, and reveal to the Father his consciousness of guilt. Thus there is a natural transition from the 'confession in crisis', characteristic of the asylum, to the Freudian dialogue, in which the analyst listens to and translates the language of unreason, but in which madness is still forced to see itself as a disobedience and a transgression. Finally, Foucault intimates, it is because psychoanalysis has refused to suppress the family structure as the only one through which madness can be seen or known that its introduction of a dialogue with madness leads to no understanding of the voices of unreason.

But this facile association of the words 'bourgeois' and 'family' has no historical justification, nor indeed is it clear that the bourgeois family has always had the most paternalistic or authoritarian structure, as families go. By this association Foucault is able to suggest that the family structure is as dispensable as the particular social structure which gives precedence to the bourgeoisie – which is surely both historically and logically a simple fallacy. If the family is always with us, is it surprising that it leaves its traces in the psychological deformities of those who are deranged? How can this fact be used as a measure either of the value of family life or of the truth of any particular conception of mental illness?

The Order of Things (a translation of *Les Mots et Les Choses*) goes one stage further in every direction than the earlier work: the sources are more recondite, the ideas more obscure and the argument more difficult to follow. It is subtitled 'an archaeology of the human sciences' and concludes with the view that 'man' is a recent invention, doomed to disappear. It is only since the Renaissance that the fact of being a *man* (rather than, say, a farmer, a soldier or a nobleman) has been given the special significance we now attribute to it. The sciences that have taken man as their object are recent inventions, already outmoded as forms of knowledge. The idea of man is as fragile and transient as any other idea in the history of human knowledge, and must give way under the impulse of a new 'experience' of the world to something we cannot name.

But are Foucault's theories really as ambitious and surprising as he makes them sound, and are the facts on which they are based so difficult to unearth? We are told, for example, that the Renaissance saw the world in terms of resemblance, but that later this '*episteme*' was replaced by another, that of 'identity and difference'. But every application of a concept can be described as the discovery of a resemblance. How, then, can resemblance cease to be a fundamental form of human knowledge? And how can it be replaced by identity and difference, with which it is inter-definable? These logical difficulties lie at the heart of Foucault's theory, and however brilliant the rhetoric, they cannot be thought away.

The Triumph of Nothingness

(*The Times*, 1984)

The Listener has recently carried a series entitled 'The Return of Grand Theory', introducing the reader to such thinkers as Gadamer, Foucault, Habermas and Althusser. Interestingly, half the articles either begin or end by protesting that the thinker in question is *not* an exponent of grand theory, or indeed of any theory at all, while judging him, all the same, to be of supreme intellectual importance.

Reading these articles came as a depressing reminder of the ease with which intellectual achievements may be discarded. Anglo-American philosophers are constantly reproached for not considering the works of Gadamer et al., when the truth is that we *have* considered them, and judged them to be largely worthless. It sounds arrogant to say it, and would that Russell were alive, that it might be said more rudely. But, so that it shall be on the public record, I shall say it now.

Most of the thinkers urged upon us as 'correctives' to our Anglo-Saxon parochialism are, in my view, charlatans of the first order, who prefer paradox and posturing to the hard-won insights of philosophical argument. Their reputation is derived from two extraneous circumstances: first, their gobbledegook, which offers to the second-rate academic an impenetrable cloak of false expertise; second, their conclusions, which are almost invariably 'subversive of the established order', in a way that dignifies the gestures of armchair rebellion whereby the academic reminds himself that he was once alive. In short, they provide to the intellectually balding a dashing wig of long hair.

Consider Althusser, the most influential and the most difficult-seeming of the grand theorists. A philosopher in a British university would probably fail an examinee who wrote like this:

> This is not just its situation in *principle* (the one it occupies in the hierarchy of instances in relation to the determinant instance: in society, the economy) nor just its situation *in fact* (whether, in the phase under consideration, it is dominant or subordinate) but *the relation of this situation in fact to this situation in principle*, that is, the very relation which makes of this situation in fact a *variation of the* – '*invariant*' – *structure, in dominance, of the totality.*

A British academic would try to teach his students to see that such a passage not only says nothing but is also *designed* to say nothing. From blocks of abstractions it erects an impassable barrier, behind which its nothingness may be concealed. Althusser's *For Marx* is composed entirely of such boxes of fortified emptiness, and it is not surprising that his disciples can agree only about the meaning of the title: Althusser is very definitely for Marx, not against him. The depressing thing is that, had he been against Marx, he would have been greeted with the derision that he deserves. Only the assurance of his impeccable political credentials enabled him to succeed; but that alone was sufficient.

The style of the charlatan is a style without hesitation. Seldom in Althusser's text will you find words like 'perhaps' or 'possibly'; nowhere will you find any serious engagement with points of view other than those approved by the author. Althusser defers to only one other human being, but his deference is total and idolatrous. That human being is Marx, and Althusser impresses on his reader that *Capital* has the status of a sacred text, which can be understood only by those who already believe it. 'It is not possible to read *Capital* properly,' he writes, 'without the help of Marxist philosophy, which must itself be read, and simultaneously, in *Capital* itself.' In other words, those who are against me do not understand me, and those who understand me know that I am right. The sentiment, like the language, is one that a British philosopher would regard himself duty-bound to subvert.

I do not say that Althusser's text is entirely without theory. But, as he says, 'this theory is the materialist dialectic, which is none other than dialectic materialism'. The neophyte, contemplating such utterances, is likely to be overcome by a certain awe. They have the same vertiginous effect as Stalin's pleonasm: 'the theories of Marx are true because they are correct.' Indeed, the more tautological an utterance, the more does it induce that state of readiness which is the prelude to unquestioning faith.

Althusser shows how gobbledegook may be regarded as wisdom, so long as it has a left-wing tone of voice. Indeed, gobbledegook like Althusser's, which shrouds left-wing dogma in an impenetrable darkness, will at once be given a place of supreme academic authority. Enclosed by Althusser's dark, the dogmatist is protected from every opposition, consoled in the belief that he cannot be threatened by that which he has learned not to see. If we use Althusser's language, then the possibility that Marxism might be mistaken cannot even be stated! Thank God that some British academics still regard it as their duty to frame their arguments in a language of which their opponents might equally avail themselves, and try also to open their students' eyes to the reality of disagreement. But for how long will their efforts be successful if the 'grand theorists' dominate the syllabus? I wonder.

Freud and Fraud

(*The Times*, 1986)

If we really wish to explain the increase in crime, we should consider the following hypothesis: that crime is explained by our desire to explain it. As we look for the causes of our behaviour, so we take attention away from the act itself, fencing it round with excuses, isolating it from judgement and making inaccessible the only ground in which the seeds of morality can be sown: the ground of individual responsibility. Surely it is this habit of explanation – this obsession with the 'genealogy' of our acts and intentions – which has most effectively 'transvalued' our values. That which Nietzsche so joyfully recommended is precisely what, in retrospect, we have greatest reason to deplore: the destruction of morality by the habit of explaining it.

It would be wrong to assume, however, that the new 'sciences' of man really *do* explain our behaviour. Their scientific guise is often no more than a mask, behind which a more serious moral purpose advances: the purpose of lowering the price of absolution. Left to his own in a godless universe, modern man sees no reason to deny himself and desires only the excuses that will justify him in the eyes of creatures like himself. And since he recognizes no authority higher than science, it is to science that he turns for his exculpation. The sciences that are chosen as his idols are those which are most prodigal of excuses, which rain down upon him a stream of whitewashing explanations and which tell him in one and the same breath that he deserves our sympathy and that he cannot be blamed.

Perhaps no science has been a more powerful source of absolution than the psychoanalysis of Freud. Here, in a single theory, the wandering conscience finds a complete kit for survival in a demoralized world. The sinner becomes a patient, and if he seems to do wrong, it is not really he who does it but an Unconscious whose machinations are unknown to him. If he is tormented by conscience, then this too is the work of the Unconscious, which erects before his inner eye the spectre of a Super Ego whose authority can be instantly discounted as the survival of a primitive fear.

As the stage of personality is vacated by responsibility, however, it becomes the scene of a new and more spectacular drama – a noble tragedy in which the self is justified in the very act of being overwhelmed. Psychoanalysis simultaneously removes the individual from the sphere of praise and blame and returns him to it vindicated, a hero who has been finally justified by the fate to which he must succumb. And psychoanalysis does all this without the slightest moral penalty: the only cost is financial, and who would not part with money for the sake of a clean conscience and an inexhaustible store of new excuses?

Of course, there has been no shortage of critics anxious to point to the scientific deficiencies of psychoanalytic theory: its dependence on metaphor, myth and imagery; its blithe indifference to evidence and refutation; its lack of experimental method; its self-serving definition of 'illness', 'therapy' and 'cure'. However, devotees of this 'science' are impatient with such feeble, external criticism. Their attitude is typified by Freud, who, presented with a dream that seemed to refute his wish-fulfilment theory, replied: 'No, your dream is an expression of the unconscious wish to refute my theory.' For the whole purpose of these pseudo-sciences of the soul is to make their exponents and their adepts *immune from criticism*, even from the criticism that their scientific pretension invites.

To break into this charmed circle and rescue the trapped moral sense is no easy task. One method, however, promises success: this is to treat the science of the soul as it treats morality, to search for its genealogy and so to 'transvalue' it. As Ernest Gellner shows in a brilliant book (*The Psychoanalytic Movement*), the result is the downfall of every claim to authority that the Freudians have made. Professor Gellner describes the genesis of Freudian psychology in modern man's most dominating fear: the fear of other people. The Freudian doctrines, he argues, are superstitious responses to that fear, which enclose it, nurture it and promise a final redemption.

The idea of an Unconscious is introduced in order to devalue all certainties and to place the patient's psyche outside of his own reach. The analyst thereby becomes priest in a solemn *rite de passage,* conducting the patient from unbelief to holy enlightenment. Gellner describes powerfully, and in the most brightly coloured prose, the causality of Freudian dogma in this concealed religious urge. In doing so he destroys its scientific claims and devalues its morality. But he also praises, in a manner that is at once serious and ironical, these novel certainties so neatly tailored to the modern conscience and so carefully separated from every suggestion of blame.

Gellner stops short, however, of drawing the most important conclusion. While this modern superstition erodes the moral sense, the religion on which our civilization was built did just the opposite, upholding and supporting the idea of moral responsibility and giving divine authority to its absolute commands. The secular superstitions offer excuses where religion offered fear, anger and blame; and while it compelled man against his will to be good, they entice him along the path of immorality. When laws are made, institutions governed and even churches led by those in the grip of these exculpating idolatries, should we really be surprised that the people turn more cheerfully to crime?

If Only Chomsky Had Stuck to Syntax

(Wall Street Journal, 2006)

Noam Chomsky's popularity owes little or nothing to the eminent place that he occupies in the world of ideas.That place was won many years ago in the science of linguistics, and no expert in the subject would, I think, dispute Professor Chomsky's title to it.

He swept away at a stroke the attempts of Ferdinand de Saussure and his followers to identify meaning through the surface structure of signs, as well as the belief, once prevalent among animal ethologists, that language could be acquired by making piecemeal connections between symbols and things. He argued that language is an all-or-nothing affair, that we are equipped by evolution with the categories needed to acquire it, and that these categories govern the 'deep structure' of our discourse, no matter what language we learn. Sentences emerge by the repeated operations of a 'transformational grammar' that translates deep structure into surface sequences: as a result, all of us are able to understand indefinitely many sentences, just as soon as we have acquired the basic linguistic competence. Language skills are essentially creative, and the infinite reach of our understanding also betokens an infinite reach in what we can mean.

Although some of those ideas had been foreseen by the pioneers of modern logic, Professor Chomsky develops them with an imaginative flair that is entirely his own. He has the true scientist's ability to translate abstract theory into concrete observation, and to discover intellectual problems where others see only ordinary facts. 'Has', I say, but perhaps 'had' would be more accurate. For Professor Chomsky long ago cast off his academic gown and donned the mantle of the prophet. For several decades now he has been devoting his energies to denouncing his native country, usually before packed halls of fans who couldn't care a fig about the theory of syntax. And many of his public appearances are in America: the only country in the whole world that rewards those who denounce it with the honours and opportunities that make denouncing it into a rewarding way of life. It is proof of Professor Chomsky's success that his diatribes are distributed by his American publishers around the world, so as to end up in the hands of America's critics everywhere – Venezuela's President Hugo Chávez included.

To his supporters Noam Chomsky is a brave and outspoken champion of the oppressed against a corrupt and criminal political class. But to his opponents he is a self-important ranter whose one-sided vision of politics is chosen for its ability to shine a spotlight on himself. And it is surely undeniable that his habit of excusing or passing over the faults of America's enemies, in order to pin all crime on his native country, suggests that he has invested more in his posture of accusation than he has invested in the truth.

To describe this posture as 'adolescent' is perhaps unfair: after all, there are plenty of quite grown-up people who believe that American foreign policy since the Second World War has been founded on a mistaken conception of America's role in the world. And it is true that we all make mistakes – so that Professor Chomsky's erstwhile support for regimes that no one could endorse in retrospect, like that of Pol Pot, is no proof of wickedness. But then the mistakes of American foreign policy are no proof of wickedness either.

This is important. For it is his ability to excite not just contempt for American foreign policy but a lively sense that it is guided by some kind of criminal conspiracy that provides the motive for Professor Chomsky's unceasing diatribes and the explanation of his influence. The world is full of people who wish to think ill of America. And most of them would like to be Americans. The Middle East seethes with such people, and Professor Chomsky appeals directly to their envious emotions, as well as to the resentments of leaders like President Chávez who cannot abide the sight of a freedom that they haven't the faintest idea how to produce or the least real desire to emulate.

Success breeds resentment, and resentment that has no safety valve becomes a desire to destroy. The proof of that was offered on 9/11 and by just about every utterance that has emerged from the Islamists since. But Americans don't want to believe it. They trust others to take the kind of pleasure in American success that they, in turn, take in the success of others. But this pleasure in others' success, which is the great virtue of America, is not to be witnessed in those who denounce her. They hate America not for her faults but for her virtues, which cast a humiliating light on those who cannot adapt to the modern world or take advantage of its achievements.

Professor Chomsky is an intelligent man. Not everything he says by way of criticizing his country is wrong. However, he is valued not for his truths but for his rage, which stokes the rage of his admirers. He feeds the self-righteousness of America's enemies, who feed the self-righteousness of Professor Chomsky. And in the ensuing blaze everything is sacrificed, including the constructive criticism that America so much needs, and that America – unlike its enemies, Professor Chomsky included – is prepared to listen to.

PART SEVEN

The West and the Rest

In Memory of Iran

(*The Times*, 1984)

Who remembers Iran? Who remembers, that is, the shameful stampede of Western journalists and intellectuals to the cause of the Iranian revolution? Who remembers the hysterical propaganda campaign waged against the Shah, the lurid press reports of corruption, police oppression, palace decadence, constitutional crisis? Who remembers the thousands of Iranian students in Western universities enthusiastically absorbing the fashionable Marxist nonsense purveyed to them by armchair radicals, so as one day to lead the campaign of riot and mendacity that preceded the Shah's downfall?

Who remembers the behaviour of those students who held as hostage the envoys of the very same power which had provided their 'education'? Who remembers Edward Kennedy's accusation that the Shah had presided over 'one of the most oppressive regimes in history' and had stolen 'umpteen billions of dollars from Iran'?

And who remembers the occasional truth that our journalists enabled us to glimpse, concerning the Shah's real achievements: his successes in combatting the illiteracy, backwardness and powerlessness of his country, his enlightened economic policy, the reforms which might have saved his people from the tyranny of evil mullahs, had he been given the chance to accomplish them? Who remembers the freedom and security in which journalists could roam Iran, gathering the gossip that would fuel their fanciful stories of a reign of terror?

True, the Shah was an autocrat. But autocracy and tyranny are not the same. An autocrat may preside, as the Shah sought to preside, over a representative parliament, over an independent judiciary, even over a free press and an autonomous university. The Shah, like Kemal Atatürk, whose vision he shared, regarded his autocracy as the means to the creation and protection of such institutions. Why did no one among the Western political scientists trouble to point this out, or to rehearse the theory which tells us to esteem not just the democratic process but also the representative and limiting institutions that may still flourish in its absence? Why did no one enjoin us to compare the political system of Iran with that of Iraq or Syria?

Why did our political scientists rush to embrace the Iranian revolution, despite the evidence that revolution in these circumstances must be the prelude to massive social disorder and a regime of terror? Why did the Western intelligentsia go on repeating the myth that the Shah was to blame for this revolution, when both Khomeini and the Marxists had been planning it for 30 years and had found, despite their many attempts to put it into operation, only spasmodic popular support?

The answer to all those questions is simple. The Shah was an ally of the West, whose achievement in establishing limited monarchy in a vital strategic region had helped to guarantee our security, to bring stability to the Middle East and to deter Soviet expansion. The Shah made the fatal mistake of supposing that the makers of Western opinion would love him for creating conditions that guaranteed their freedom. On the contrary, they hated him. The Shah had reckoned without the great death wish that haunts our civilization and which causes its vociferous members to propagate any falsehood, however absurd, provided only that it damages our chances of survival.

For a while, of course, those vociferous elements will remain silent on the embarrassing topic of Iran, believing that the collapse of Iranian institutions, the establishment of religious terror, the Soviet expansion into Afghanistan and the end of stability in the region are all due to some other cause than the

Iranian revolution. Those who lent their support to this tragedy simply turned their back on it and went elsewhere, to prepare a similar outcome for the people of Turkey, Nicaragua, El Salvador, Chile, South Africa – or wherever else our vital interests may be damaged.

Of course, it is difficult now for a Western correspondent to enter Iran, and if he did so, it would not be fun. He could not, like the ghouls who sent their dispatches from Beirut, adopt a public posture of the front-line hero. He would have to witness, quietly and in terror of his life, things that beggar description: the spontaneous 'justice' of the revolutionary guards, the appalling scenes of violence, torture and demonic frenzy, the public humiliation of women, the daily sacrifice of lives too young to be conscious of the meaning for which they are condemned to destruction.

He would also have to confront the truth which has been staring him in the face for years, and which he could still recognize had the habit of confessing to his errors been preserved: the truth that limited monarchy is the *right* form of government for Iran, which can be saved only by the restoration of the Shah's legitimate successor. But such a result would be in the interests not only of the Iranian people but also of the West. Hence few Western journalists are likely to entertain it.

The Lesson of Lebanon

(*The Times*, 1985)

Those who visited Lebanon 20 years ago will recall a thriving, prosperous – if somewhat seedy – community in a region of poverty and war. To arrive there from the 'United Arab Republic' of Egypt and Syria was to pass from suspicion and tyranny to lawful government, free opinion and religious toleration. To achieve such conditions in the dismembered fragments of the Ottoman Empire has never been easy. To achieve them in a country where Christian and Muslim, Maronite, Armenian and Orthodox, Sunni, Druze and Shia lived side by side, honourably bound to the ancient customs that distinguish them, was one of the most remarkable results in modern times of true political culture.

This political culture would not have existed but for the Christians of Lebanon, who brought to government a respect for law and a spirit of willing negotiation. This spirit was shared by the Sunni Muslims, and it was from the bargain struck between these two communities that the constitution emerged, guaranteeing the rights of Christians and ensuring to them a decisive influence in government. The constitution was in some ways inequitable. But it was a constitution, and it permitted that most precious of political achievements and one absent from much for the region: a rule of law.

The Christians of Lebanon are long established, their title to their land being far older than that of the Muslims. The Maronite Church is in communion with Rome and retains in its liturgy the ancient Syriac language that was spoken by

Christ. Its congregation is spread through town, village and country, through every class and profession and through every political posture. Such privileges as the Christians have enjoyed were purchased by their trade and industry, and their success has enriched their Muslim neighbours as well as themselves.

Until recently these people, many of them descended from the earliest Christians, who have kept the faith alive in biblical lands, had the support and sympathy of every Christian nation. When they were threatened with extinction, as in 1860, their cry rang through Christendom with an imperative reverberation.

Now all that has changed. Syria, armed by the Soviet Union, governed by a single party and obedient to a harsh dictator, has imposed its will on Lebanon. Syria has occupied, and continues to occupy, half of the country – a fact that causes no comment in the West, where only Israel's misdeeds are noticed. Through Syrian auspices the Palestine Liberation Organization (PLO) was introduced into Lebanon, with the purpose of destabilizing a peaceful community. The Muslim sects were divided, first from the Christians and then from each other. Training camps for international terrorists were established: the area was filled with refugees and with the bloodthirsty journalists who dog their footsteps. And at last the invasion was provoked which, however justified, was to call down the wrath of the media upon Israel.

Having achieved all this, the Syrians dismissed the PLO, liquidated its garrisons and now, through evil-minded proxies, are moving towards a final solution of the problem posed by a people who depended on their protection and who also wrought their will.

Throughout these events the Christians have endeavoured to sustain the legal order of Lebanon. Two enemies have frustrated their efforts: the Syrian state and Western journalists, who have acted in character as the fifth column of dictatorial power. It is a truth obvious to all but the journalist that his ability to report on a country's troubles is a proof of its civic virtue. A real tyranny excludes the journalist from its territory, or else permits him to enter only on terms that are dictated by itself. It is precisely such tyrannies that, acting by proxy in the free states where the journalist wanders, attract his attention by a trail of blood and lay the blame for the deaths which he discovers at the door of the only power that he may safely criticize.

By such methods the Syrians have been able to persuade the Western public that the Shia Muslims of Lebanon – stirred into unwonted cruelty and ignorant fanaticism – are a major force, expressing an old, justly founded grievance. At the same time the public has learned to distance itself from the Christians, whose achievements and destiny ought to be its major concern. Having established a rule of law and permitted criticism, the Christians are blamed for the lawlessness of those who acknowledge no aims or interests but their own.

Thus when a Christian militia attacked the Palestinian camps, it was rightly condemned, and a political crisis was provoked from which Israel and the Lebanese Christians have failed to recover. The same camps were subsequently surrounded by Syria's Shia proxies and their populations exposed to heartless massacre. However, not a word is said. Not only is the journalist now excluded from the bloody transaction; he knows that if he is to stay at his post he needs the protection of the gangsters responsible.

An even greater cost would be paid by the journalist who reported truthfully what has happened to the 4,500 Lebanese Christian soldiers held in the concentration camp at Mazze, in Syria, or to the innocent Christian villagers of Saida and Jezzine area, now encircled by Syrian-backed forces who wish to drive them from the land which they have occupied since before the birth of the Prophet. Between March and April of this year, according to reliable reports, 60 of their villages were destroyed, 8,500 of their houses burned, 12,000 of their number made homeless, 80 churches pillaged or destroyed, 17 convents razed and 200 people murdered in cold blood.

Christian nations have been offered many a *casus belli* by Lebanon's Shia Muslim fanatics, and not only by the leader who, while dedicating himself to the expulsion of justice from his homeland, rejoiced in the title of minister for justice. However, thanks to the journalists and to the diplomats whom they influence, the challenge will never be accepted. All the same, let us hope that those in the West who call themselves Christians will remember in their prayers a people who have kept alive, at such cost to themselves, the memory of Christ in lands that we should still call holy, had holiness retained its meaning for us.

Decent Debate Mustn't Be the Victim

(Daily Mail, 2006)

Last night the BBC and Channel 4 showed the now notorious newspaper cartoons of Muhammad. That their decisions to do so will further enflame Muslims throughout the world is not in doubt. But does the understandable fury these cartoons have elicited mean that they should never have been published or broadcast?

There is no easy answer. But the fact is that our predominantly Christian society in the West is now so sceptical about religion that we no longer know how to deal with this bitter controversy. We can't rely on the old-fashioned rule of common courtesy, which says that you must treat religion – whether your own or another's – with respect, and neither laugh at its icons nor blaspheme against its gods. Courtesy is a dwindling commodity in modern societies, and besides, in our growing scepticism, we in Britain have assumed that religion is no more than a superficial gloss on life, as easy for a Muslim to discard as it is for someone brought up in the dwindling faiths of Europe. And when we suddenly see that our superficial attitude might offend the very soul of the Muslim community, we rush to excuse ourselves by trying to pass stupid and draconian laws such as the ragbag Race and Religious Hatred Bill, which was rightly mauled in the Commons on Tuesday. And, in doing so, we happily prepare to jettison the most important legacies of our civilization, including free speech and open debate, simply because we have not had the courtesy to use them wisely.

In this way, our society takes a step towards totalitarianism, while silencing the debate that it most needs now to have – the debate concerning the terms on which Muslims, Christians, Jews and unbelievers can coexist as citizens. Of course it was wrong to publish those cartoons – as wrong as it would be to publish a cartoon of the Virgin Mary in a bikini, or of Christ in a clinch with the Magdalene. On the other hand, the Christian religion is routinely exposed to these insults. Blasphemous accounts of the life of Christ win prizes at film festivals, images of the cross pickled in urine or of the Virgin composed of elephant dung are unsurprising products of Young British Art. And although these things shock us, and we turn away from them in sadness and disgust, we do not cry out for vengeance against their perpetrators. Nor do we believe that the law should punish them. Maybe this is because our religious belief is now too weak to stir in us. But it is also a reminder that we are living in a society rotten with disrespect.

The remedy must come through reminding people of the rules of good behaviour. We need to understand that icons and rituals are holy things, and that it is our duty to respect them, even when – especially when – we regard them as ridiculous. This discipline is hard, and I confess that I have often strayed from it. But it is the precondition of peaceful coexistence. This does not mean that we should not criticize another's religion or mention the unpalatable truths about its followers. On the contrary, there can be no accommodation between Muslim and Christian culture if we surround all points of disagreement with a veil of frightened silence. I'm ashamed that Christians established the Inquisition, pillaged Constantinople and the Holy Land, and imposed colonial systems of government in Muslim lands.

I expect Muslims to challenge me about these things, and I know I must be prepared to discuss them and to show, if I can, that they are deviations from the Christian message.

But then, Muslims should reciprocate. Murder, pillage and conquest have been part of their legacy too, and we urgently need to hear them acknowledge these crimes and also repudiate them as violations of their faith. The purpose of the debate is not to score points but to remind each other of our shared humanity and its imperfections, and of the need for courtesy and respect if we are to live together as citizens. Although it was wrong to publish and broadcast cartoons that every Muslim will find offensive, it was also understandable.

We cannot turn a blind eye to the fact that the London suicide bombers were Muslims who saw themselves as *mujahideen*, advancing the cause of their faith. If a Christian were to blow innocent bystanders to smithereens as part of a crusade against the heathen, no doubt we would see cartoons of Christ with a fuse attached, and crosses turned to daggers. Christians, too, would find this offensive. But if you respect the icons, the rituals and the sacred texts of another person's faith, you can raise even the most intimate questions as to its truth and its moral record without causing offence. Indeed, if you look at the works of Islamic philosophers down the centuries, you will find just such an intense interrogation of the faith – one conducted under strict laws of respect towards the name and the person of Muhammad, but exposing every article of faith to rational interrogation. You find a similar tradition of critical inquiry in Christian philosophy too, and also in the Jewish Talmud.

Politeness and decency are second nature to anyone truly brought up on the teachings of the Koran. So are other virtues that we are losing in modern Christian societies: respect for the sacredness of life, temperance, the care of the elderly and family values. The decline of the Christian faith in this country has gone hand in hand with the loss of those values. And this is one reason why Christians need to debate their faith with Muslims, to understand where they differ and to rediscover the virtues that they share.

So long as this debate is silenced by draconian laws, we will be tempted to see jihad written over every Muslim face, and Muslims will see moral ignorance written over the faces of those who do not share their faith. The remedy for this is not to outlaw discussion but to promote the courtesy that makes discussion possible.

The Wrong Way to Treat President Putin

(*Forbes*, 2014)

With characteristic blindness to its real situation the European Union has responded to the seizure of Crimea by imposing 'sanctions' on the Russian hierarchy. The mafia bosses who surround and depend on President Putin are no longer to be allowed to travel to their villas in Tuscany or to draw on their extensive European bank accounts. Heart-broken mistresses in luxury hotels will go unvisited for months on end, unless they invite one of the Eurocrats from the restaurant downstairs. Mansions in Mayfair will remain shuttered until the stucco begins to crumble, and struggling football teams and racehorses will look in vain for a purchaser. That this will make the faintest difference to Russia's expansionist foreign policy is an illusion of staggering naivety. More important, however, is the deep ignorance of history that this measure reveals.

For let us look back to the collapse of the Soviet Union in the time of the wily Mr Gorbachev. Why was it that, all of a sudden and with no real forewarning, the Soviet elite relinquished the reins of power and quietly backed away from government? The answer is simple: because it was in their interest to do so. Thanks to President Reagan's strategy and the North Atlantic Alliance, it had become apparent that it would not be possible to seize the assets that lay to the west of the Soviet Empire by force. But it had also become apparent that force was no longer necessary. Over a period of 70 years the Soviet Union had built up a system of espionage and underground banking that essentially conferred on the KGB elite more or less complete freedom of movement on the continent of Europe and a secure system of private finance. Already in 1989 the high-ranking officers who took the leading decisions owned property in the West and had transferred their share of the assets stolen over decades from the Russian people to their Swiss bank accounts.

They then perceived that the process could be completed at no extra cost. By privatizing the Soviet economy to themselves, and adopting a mask of democratic government, the elite backed out of communism into the world of the glitterati. They were now free citizens of the world, able to travel, to own property, to draw on their stolen billions and play with their own private football teams. How stupid they had been all those years, to go along with the legacy of communist paranoia, and to believe that their role as alpha-males depended on threatening, invading, subverting and tormenting, when the whole thing could be achieved by being nice!

So what happened? With a few leads from Gorbachev the KGB got the message. Privatize your own little bit of the Soviet economy, and if necessary imprison your competitors for tax evasion. Draw a lifelong salary from your share of the stolen assets. Secure your mansion in London, your account in Switzerland and your yacht in the Mediterranean, and pose as a businessman, with interests in gas and oil. Pursue a career of social climbing and erotic adventure in the West, and leave the old monotowns of Russia to crumble to dust.

Of course, it was an unseemly spectacle, though not so unseemly that the German elite were repelled by it. On the contrary, by inviting former German Chancellor Gerhard Schröder onto the board of Gazprom, Putin made the German Social Democrats part of the game. All across Europe the KGB elite has been able to call on favours received, and to buy its way into a society already rotten with underhand dealing. And the result, disgusting though it undeniably is, does not compare unfavourably with the previous situation, in which the same elite retained power by oppressing the Russian people, imprisoning Eastern Europe and stirring violent conflict all across the world.

So what will be the effect of the proposed sanctions? Note that they target individuals, not the Russian state. They are expressly designed to imprison the Russian oligarchs once again in the country that they ruined, and from which they escaped with flatulent sighs of relief a quarter of a century ago. That would be a viable strategy if the European Union had the military means to contain the oligarchs behind the Russian border. That was the strategy of President Reagan, which was abandoned by Obama when he decided not to proceed with the missile defence system that had been proposed for Eastern Europe, and which in any case has never had the wholehearted endorsement of either France or Germany.

So we are back where we started: a powerful menagerie of snarling alpha–males, confined behind bars that will give way at the first determined shake of them. And it is only a matter of time before the shaking will begin. Peace between Russia and the West was secured when the self-interest of the Russian oligarchs required it. But it is no longer so clear that peace is in their interest, and to assume that they will respect the interests of anyone else is to show an amazing disregard for their recent history.

Why Iraq Is a Write-Off

(Forbes, 2014)

In 1915 a couple of minor diplomats, the Englishman Sir Mark Sykes and the Frenchman François George-Picot, began negotiating to divide the Ottoman Empire, which had entered the Great War on the side of Germany. In 1916 the Sykes–Picot agreement was signed by France, Britain and Russia. By the end of the war Russia was out of the game, following the Bolshevik Revolution, and Atatürk was busy saving the Turkish-speaking remnant of the Ottoman Empire. Britain and France had a free hand to divide the Arab lands between them. They drew weird boundary lines supposedly corresponding to the 'nations' of the region. They even appointed sovereigns to some of them, drawing on a bank of Arab pretenders among whom the Hashemite tribe were prominent. And they administered these territories under a 'mandate' granted by the League of Nations.

Of the new nation-states only Lebanon and Egypt had any real claims to national identity. Both had large Christian populations – in Lebanon possibly a majority. And both had a long history of defiance towards the Sultan in Istanbul. It should have been obvious that the other territories in the region – which we now know as Iraq, Syria, Jordan and Palestine – were neither nations nor viable states but simply places on the map. Iraq was put together from a population divided between a Shi'ite majority and Sunni minority, with a sizeable scattering of Christians, and a large population of Kurdish-speaking Sunnis. Its boundaries, like those of Syria, had little historical foundation, and – with the exception of the Kurds, who are fiercely nationalistic – the

Iraqi people defined themselves in terms of their faith, not in terms of their national identity.

We in the West have inherited a form of identity that is largely unknown in the Arab world. We identify ourselves in terms of our country and its law. This law is secular, man-made and changeable. We owe allegiance to the nation, and we include within the nation people of different faiths and different family ties. In the Arab world people have not, on the whole, identified themselves in that way. Sunni Muslims have only a weak attachment to territory and a marked reluctance to view themselves as tied to their neighbours of differing faith by binding obligations. The secular law of the nation-state has only a vacillating authority for them, since they regard themselves as governed by another and eternal law, laid down by God through the mouth of the Prophet. Their language is a universal language, attached to no specific territory, and their faith is a universal faith, which tells them that they belong to no particular place or time but to the universal *ummah* of the faithful. In other words, their faith confers on them an identity that is not a national identity and which is indeed incompatible with secular law and national boundaries.

Not surprisingly, therefore, places like Iraq and Syria have been places of constant conflict, stable only when some usurping army officer or ruthless dynasty has been able to seize control, as happened with Saddam Hussein in Iraq, and Hafez al-Assad in Syria. Both of those unsavoury characters retained control by means of the Ba'ath ('resurrection') party, which had shaped itself on Leninist principles and exerted a terroristic control over the people through the operations of the secret police. Both countries were without legal opposition or a true rule of law. It was only natural that they should enter into conflict with their neighbours and with the wider world.

But this is where everything went wrong. President George W. Bush imagined that, by deposing Saddam, he would open the way to a new and democratic Iraq. This was to make two incredibly naive assumptions: first, that democracy is the default position in politics, and second, that you can achieve democracy even where there is no genuine nation-state.

History tells us that the default position in politics is priest-haunted tyranny, and that democracy is achieved only by enormous efforts and usually not without extended periods of civil war, such as marked the English seventeenth century or the American nineteenth century. Democracy comes about when people lay down their arms and agree to live with each other on terms, negotiating with those they dislike for a share of the action. A democrat is a person who agrees to be governed by someone from a different faith, a different tribe, a different family or interest group, a different worldview. What makes a democrat possible? The answer is: the nation. When you and I define our loyalty in national terms, we can put aside all differences of religion, tribe and ethnicity, and submit to a shared system of law. We participate in the making of that law, and agree to be bound by it, because it is our law, which operates over the territory that is ours. We have made a home together, and set aside our divisions in order to settle side by side.

That process never occurred in the Arab world, or if it did, only in fragile and unstable instances, such as Lebanon. The assumption that, because Iraq exists on the map, it exists as a nation-state, with a true national identity, and that Iraqis will stand up for their nation and fight for its existence – that assumption was and is patently ridiculous. No sooner did ISIS appear over the horizon than the Iraqi troops abandoned their arms and their uniforms and fled back to their native villages. They behaved like a mercenary army conscripted by a foreign power. Which is essentially what they were. Of course, they will fight for their religion – but their religion precisely divides them from other Iraqis, and cannot serve as a unifying force.

Only one community in Iraq has responded as we might to the invasion by ISIS, and that is the Kurdish community, which has been able to carve out a semi-autonomous region. Why is this? Surely the answer is clear. Being a Kurd is a matter of language, history and an ancestral claim to territory. It is a proto-national, rather than a religious, identity. Hence when Kurds fight, they fight for their country rather than their faith. And an emerging Kurdistan is likely to be the only peaceful fragment of the Iraq made in Britain and America. Let us hope that it becomes an ally of the West in the region. For it will probably be the only ally we have.

PART EIGHT

Cultural Corruption

The Art of Motor-Cycle Maintenance

(*The Times*, 1984)

People need things, almost as much as things need people. The critical moment of their mutual support is the moment of breakdown. Suddenly, the object on which everything depended – the car, the boiler, the drain or the dinner suit – is unusable, and you contemplate its betrayal in helpless unbelief. It is some time before you overcome your self-pity enough to recognize that its need is greater than yours. But where do you turn for the person who will assist it? This question, the most irksome faced by civilized man, is constantly posed by my pathetically dependent motor bike.

Time was when everything usable was also repairable: chairs, sofas, carts, hats, accordions, carpets, all were in a state of flux, as new defects revealed themselves and new patches were affixed to cover them. Objects entered the world of human users only to pass at once from Being to Becoming.

Repair was not so much a habit as an honoured custom. People respected the past of damaged things, restored them as though healing a child and looked on their handiwork with satisfaction. In the act of repair the object was made anew, to occupy the social position of the broken one. Worn shoes went to the anvil, holed socks and unravelled sleeves to the darning last – that peculiar mushroom-shaped object which stood always ready on the mantelpiece.

The custom of repair was not confined to the home. Every town, every village, had its cobbler, its carpenter, its wheelwright and its smith. In each community people supported repairers, who in turn supported things. And our surnames testify to the honour in which their occupations were held. But to where have they repaired, these people who guaranteed the friendliness of objects? With great difficulty you may still find a cobbler – but for the price of his work you could probably buy a new pair of shoes. For the cost of 15 digital watches you may sometimes find a person who will fix the mainspring of your grandfather's timepiece.

The truth is that repair, like every serious social activity, has its ethos, and when that ethos is lost, no amount of slapdash labour can make up for it. The person who repairs must love the broken object, and must love also the process of repair and all that pertains to it. The modern motor vehicle is the subject not of repair but of 'after-sales service', a euphemism implying that only the firm who made it can restore it, according to specialized procedures of its own and with a view to ensuring that it will never again be 'as good as new'.

Which returns me to my theme. Here and there you may still find places where the ethos of repair lingers, and where you will not be brushed contemptuously aside merely because your vehicle is of a model, a year or a character that falls outside some manufacturer's prescription. On Ladbroke Grove one such place still survives, a peculiar testimony to declining values, amid the planning blight of Kensal Town. Only the name – Hamrax Motors Ltd, in yellow plastic lettering – seems to unite this little Victorian terrace with its surrounding world.

Above the ruined classical mask of the shop, however, is affixed a more ancient label – an enamel plaque in royal blue, bearing the title 'Imperial Motors' – and beneath it, in the window, is a most extraordinary revelation of ancient customs. Where you would expect the chrome extravagance of the latest bum-tickler from Japan, or the polished props of the fetishist's daydream, you find only inexplicable twists of wire, dusty fuses, disordered piles of sprockets, tappets, axle nuts and cotter pins. Beyond, in the deep interior, stand shelf upon shelf of smudged cardboard boxes, each labelled with some hieroglyph and each overflowing with small metallic parts.

In the cramped counter of this shop men congregate from every corner of England: steel-studded ton-up boys from Watford, gaberdine-clad Sunbeam buffs from the depths of Devon, solitary rallyists who have bumped themselves from Wales on farmyard bikes of their own devising. With infinite patience, the eccentric need of each is catered for: a chain link for an ancient single-cylinder Matchless will be searched out with as much concern as a complete gearbox for last year's Kawasaki. Indeed, the more recondite and intricate the job, the more the staff will welcome it, and problems of repair awaken interest proportionate not to their profit but to their rarity.

Hamrax Motors consists of three terraced houses knocked together, and every corner of the dark interior is given over to the storage of motor-cycle parts, which are stacked on shelves and hung on the walls like votive offerings. To reach the workshop you must go out of the shop and down a flight of stone steps beneath an arch. This touching architectural detail, which once gave drama to the street below, typifies the shadow-filled grandeur of the Victorian slums. Alas, the rage for hygiene and social justice has left nothing standing, save only the patched fabric of Hamrax itself, sustained by the life-giving ethos of repair and by the sense that an Englishman's bike is his charger.

Temples of Anxiety

(*The Times*, 1985)

Since the Enlightenment, Western man has been prey to the pernicious superstition (as Dean Inge called it) of 'Progress'. He has been disposed to believe that all human affairs are subject to a principle of improvement and therefore that no institutions or practices ought to endure.

It is reasonable to believe that science, in the right conditions, will continuously advance. And with the advance of science come the steady mastery of nature, the improvement of technology and the conquest of disease. But scientific advance is precarious. It depends on institutions, such as universities, which owe their existence to the wisdom of supremely unprogressive epochs and their durability to a spiritual capital which they are always spending and which they seldom replace. Moreover, every scientific advance is paid for by a simultaneous retreat, as we endeavour to protect ourselves from the unforeseen consequences of our presumptuous experiments.

Nevertheless, so long as it can flourish, science is inherently progressive. The superstition lies in the belief that what is true of science is true of every other human endeavour – of politics, morality, religion and art. In those activities, which depend on an intuitive sensitivity to life and happiness, we may experience a decline, precisely when progressive thinking triumphs. For then firm instinct gives way to unfounded speculation, careful discipline to unruly freedom of choice.

In the field of aesthetics the result has been catastrophic. Art, craft and decoration have all been subjected to a tyrannical pursuit of novelty. Where previous generations have been content to accept patiently transcribed solutions to recurrent problems, we blithely and ignorantly set ourselves on another course, imagining that our superior science is also a superior wisdom and that our technical accomplishment is a substitute for art.

A case in point is the telephone booth, designed by Giles Gilbert Scott, architect of Liverpool's Anglican Cathedral. The familiar red box is one of the last creations of a disciplined tradition, whose products also include the Gothic factory, the Palladian clubhouse, the Pullman railway carriage and the Bombay shirt. The ruling idea of this tradition has been stability: certain forms, materials, details and colours have authority for us. It is from them, therefore, that we should choose the façades that will mask the latest horrifying advance of science, and so integrate it into the life that it threatens.

In every English village there is one object that stands out as the prime focus of the traveller's attention and the fitting representation of the stable government beneath whose mantle he journeys. This object is the telephone booth: a cast-iron structure in imperial red, classical in outline, but with an interesting suggestion of Bauhaus naughtiness in its fenestration. Raised on a slight plinth, and with the proportions appropriate to a column base, it is capped by a gentle pediment, beneath which a panel of opalescent glass, lit from behind, makes a kind of cornice, bearing the word 'telephone' in sober classical letters. The door, divided into three parts by its mullions, has a brass handle set into the cast-iron frame, and above the cornice a little crown is embossed, symbol of national identity and promise of enduring government. So suitable has this form proved to the streets, countryside and villages of England that it now appears on Christmas-card snowscapes, beside the Gothic spire, the gabled cottage and the five-barred gate. Only what is genuinely loved can be subjected to such a degradation.

British Telecom has, however, threatened to replace these familiar landmarks by barbarous concoctions of steel and aluminium of the kind to be seen in New York. In a sense this is only right. For the telephone testifies to the moral reality of Progress. Human beings were never meant to separate themselves so far from those they love as to take pleasure in their disembodied voices. They were never meant to conduct their business so rapidly that letters cease to be effective. They were never meant to start up nervously at the ringing of a mere machine, or to give it precedence over every human contact.

The telephone is the vessel of anxiety. At the same time, therefore, the booths are really temples, dedicated to a ruling deity. The smell of stale cigarette ash and rusting iron has become, for us, like the smell of incense – the record of long, holy moments, in which the god Anxiety has reached down to us with a personal concern. To have confined so cruel a god within so pleasant a temple is not the meanest achievement of the classical concept of design. At the same time, the burden of Progress has been lightened. The traditional booth makes the worship of Anxiety into a familiar feature of the English landscape – as familiar as the Gothic spire or the Gregorian rectory.

We must therefore insist that telephone booths be considered to be buildings within the meaning of the Town and Country Planning Acts. Like any other temple, they must be made subject to conservation orders. For although it does not matter very much how a phone booth looks in Birmingham, where modern architects have already done their work, it still matters on a village green, a hillside or a moor.

The Modern Cult of Ugliness

(*Daily Mail*, 2009)

When asked by the BBC to make a film about beauty, my first instinct was to present all the wonderful works of art and music, the magnificent buildings and landscapes, the glorious variety of animals and birds, that have shone a light of beauty in my life. To share with others these things that I love would surely bring pleasure and knowledge to my audience, as well as consolation to me – for when people share things they value, they too are comforted. But as I worked on the script, I was constantly troubled by the thought that beauty seems no longer to have the significance that once it had.

In the modern age, we are surrounded by man-made ugliness. And artists, who used to devote their efforts to idealizing the human form, to recording the charms of nature and bringing order and beauty to our sorrows, are no longer interested in those tasks. Galleries of contemporary art are filled with the debris of modern life, with subhuman figures purposefully designed to demean and desecrate the human image and with ludicrous installations that mean nothing at all.

This lapse into ugliness is nowhere more apparent or more intrusive than in the desolate city centres produced by modern architects. In the programme, I decided that I should show one of these wastelands, and so took the film crew with me to Reading, the town in whose shadow I grew up. As I looked around the centre, I recognized nothing that I had known. Gone were the lovely Victorian terrace streets, elegant public buildings and smart hotels. In their place were huge, grey, concrete slabs.

The welcoming surroundings of the old town centre had been replaced by buildings deemed to be 'useful'. And the most striking fact – which I immediately decided should form the theme of my film – was that these 'useful' buildings were, in fact, entirely useless. Constructed to house office blocks, a shopping centre, a bus station and car parks, they were now boarded up and crumbling. Walls were plastered with graffiti, and doors and windows vandalized – though I don't blame the vandals for finishing the job that the architects began.

What happened to Reading happened to Birmingham and Coventry, to Newcastle, to Liverpool and Leeds and a hundred other once beautiful towns – the wholesale demolition of genial streets and their replacement by buildings deemed to be functional, which lost their function in a matter of years. The point is that there is a deep human need for beauty, and if you ignore that need in architecture, your buildings will not last, since people will never feel at home in them. Indeed, the only beings at home in the decaying part of Reading I visited were the pigeons fouling the pavements.

This triumph of 'function' over form in recent decades has dehumanized our towns and cities. But it is not only architecture that has drifted away from beauty. Contemporary art has made a cult of ugliness, and artists vie with each other in the game of putting the human face on display and throwing dung at it. Not all artists, of course: there is still beautiful art today as there has always been. But such art remains below the horizon of official patronage.

Official art today is the art sponsored and encouraged by the likes of the wealthy collector Charles Saatchi, who championed Damien Hirst and his cadavers of cows, calves and pickled sharks. It is the art favoured by the Tate's director, Nicholas Serota – not an idealization of life but one of life's sordid offshoots, such as Tracey Emin's notorious *My Bed*, an installation of an unmade bed complete with condoms, underpants and empty vodka bottles.

We should not think that these changes in the world of art – which have been paralleled, too, in the worlds of music and literature – are without significance. What we look at, listen to and read affects us in the deepest part of our being. Once we start to celebrate ugliness, then we become ugly too. Just as art and architecture have uglified themselves, so have our manners, our relationships and our language become crude.

Without the guidance offered by beauty and good taste we find it difficult to relate to each other in a natural or graceful way. Society itself becomes fractured and atomized.

This official uglification of our world is the work of the ivory-towered elites of the liberal classes – people who have little sympathy for how the rest of us live and who, with their mania for modernizing, are happy to rip up beliefs that have stood the test of time for millennia.

What they forget is that ordinary people hunger for beauty as they have always hungered, for beauty is the voice of comfort, the voice of home.

When a lovely melody, a sublime landscape or a passage of exquisite poetry comes before your senses and your mind, you know that you are at home in the world. Beauty is the voice that settles us, the assurance that we belong among others, in a place of sharing and consolation. By contrast, the ugly art and architecture of today divides society rather than bringing it together. Written across so much of it is the word 'me'. Beauty is not popular among professional architects – it suggests a scaling down of 'artistic' pretentions for the sake of people whom they don't need to know.

The images of brutality and destruction in modern art, the tales of vicious and repugnant ways of life in today's novels, the violent and harrowing music of our age – all these are forms of egotism, ways in which insignificant people draw attention to themselves by standing ostentatiously apart from the majority of us who crave beauty. Over the decades this has produced both weariness and brutalization in society, yet the critics still go along with it. And to gain favour from the critics today, you must avoid making something beautiful.

This flies in history's face. The most sublime representations of the human form we owe to the pagan gods of antiquity.

We are in awe of those statues of Apollo and Venus which adorned ancient temples. Our tradition of painting is owed to the Church and the icons that have illuminated Christian worship. You don't have to be a religious believer to appreciate the ecstasy of a Madonna by Bellini or Raphael, or the tranquillity of a temple Buddha.

Through so much human existence art has sanctified the world, even in the eyes of those without religious faith. And when the scientific revolution of the seventeenth century cast doubt on the old Christian idea of a God-centred universe, artists sought to renew their faith through the beauty that surrounded them in the landscapes of nature. Yet, as society has become more urban and less religious, the cult of ugliness has taken hold. It can be no coincidence that it has come at a time of unprecedented prosperity. Ugly modern art is produced by the pampered children of the democratic state, who have never had to struggle, who have not known war and who have entered at the earliest age into the lap of luxury.

Maybe we can live with their rubbish – after all, we don't have to frequent the museums and galleries where it is displayed. But modern architecture is unavoidable. Nowhere do we feel the need for beauty more vividly than in these vast, supposedly functional, buildings. Without ornament, grandeur, style or dignity, a building is opaque to us. We cannot find our way around it. Nothing seems to face us, to beckon to us, to welcome us. When we enter such a building, we are immediately lost. Here we should contrast the old railway stations such as Paddington and St Pancras. The architecture is noble, serene, upright. The spaces open before you. Everything is picked out with ornamental details. You are at home here, and you have no difficulty finding the ticket office, the platform or the way through the crowds.

I end my film with a tribute to St Pancras – a performance of Pergolesi's sublime *Stabat Mater*, beautifully sung in the great arched spaces of that fine old building, made useful again by the Eurostar. Useful and loved because it is beautiful.

High Culture Is Being Corrupted
by a Culture of Fakes

(*Guardian*, 2012)

A high culture is the self-consciousness of a society. It contains the works of art, literature, scholarship and philosophy that establish a shared frame of reference among educated people. High culture is a precarious achievement, and endures only if it is underpinned by a sense of tradition and by a broad endorsement of the surrounding social norms. When those things evaporate, as inevitably happens, high culture is superseded by a culture of fakes.

Faking depends on a measure of complicity between the perpetrator and the victim, who together conspire to believe what they don't believe and to feel what they are incapable of feeling. There are fake beliefs, fake opinions, fake kinds of expertise. There is also fake emotion, which comes about when people debase the forms and the language in which true feeling can take root, so that they are no longer fully aware of the difference between the true and the false. Kitsch is one very important example of this. The kitsch work of art is not a response to the real world, but a fabrication designed to replace it. Yet producer and consumer conspire to persuade each other that what they feel in and through the kitsch work of art is something deep, important and real.

Anyone can lie. One need only have the requisite intention – in other words, to say something with the intention to deceive. Faking, by contrast, is an achievement. To fake things you have to take people in, yourself included. In an important sense, therefore, faking is not something that can be intended, even though it comes about through intentional actions. The liar can pretend to be shocked when his lies are exposed, but his pretence is merely a continuation of his lying strategy. The fake really is shocked when he is exposed, since he had created around himself a community of trust, of which he himself was a member. Understanding this phenomenon is, it seems to me, integral to understanding how a high culture works, and how it can become corrupted.

We are interested in high culture because we are interested in the life of the mind, and we entrust the life of the mind to institutions because it is a social benefit. Even if only a few people are capable of living this life to the full, we all benefit from its results, in the form of knowledge, technology, legal and political understanding, and the works of art, literature and music that evoke the human condition and also reconcile us to it. Aristotle went further, identifying contemplation (*theoria*) as the highest goal of mankind, and leisure (*schole*) as the means to it. Only in contemplation, he suggested, are our rational needs and desires properly fulfilled. Kantians might prefer to say that in the life of the mind we reach through the world of means to the kingdom of ends. We leave behind the routines of instrumental reasoning and enter a world in which ideas, artefacts and expressions exist for their own sake, as objects of intrinsic value. We are then granted the true homecoming of the spirit. Such seems to be implied by Friedrich Schiller, in his *Letters on the Aesthetic Education of Man* (1794). Similar views underlie the German romantic view of *Bildung*: self-cultivation as the goal of education and the foundation of the university curriculum.

The life of the mind has its intrinsic methods and rewards. It is concerned with the true, the beautiful and the good, which between them define the scope of reasoning and the goals of serious inquiry. But each of those goals can be faked, and one of the most interesting developments in our educational and cultural institutions over the past half-century is the extent to which fake culture and fake scholarship have driven out the true varieties. It is important to ask why.

The most important way of clearing intellectual space for fake scholarship and culture is to marginalize the concept of truth. This looks difficult at first. After all, every utterance, every discussion, seems to be aimed at truth by its very nature. How can knowledge come to us, if we are indifferent to the truth of what we read? But this is too simple. There is a way of debating that disregards the truth of another's words, since it is concerned to diagnose them, to discover 'where they are coming from', and to reveal the emotional, moral and political attitudes that underlie a given choice of words. The habit of 'going behind' your opponent's words stems from Karl Marx's theory of ideology, which tells us that, in bourgeois conditions, concepts, habits of thought and ways of seeing the world are adopted because of their socio-economic function, not their truth.

The idea of justice, for instance, which sees the world in terms of rights and responsibilities and assigns ownership and obligations across society, was dismissed by early Marxists as a piece of bourgeois 'ideology'. The ideological purpose of the concept is to validate 'bourgeois relations of production' which, from another perspective, can be seen to violate the very requirements that the concept of justice lays down. Therefore, the concept of justice is in conflict with itself, and serves merely to mask a social reality that has to be understood in other terms – in terms of the powers to which people are subject, rather than the rights that they claim.

The Marxist theory of ideology is extremely contentious, not least because it is tied to socio-economic hypotheses that are no longer believable. However, it survives in the work of Michel Foucault and other intellectuals, notably in Foucault's *The Order of Things* (1966) and in his witty essays on the origins of the prison and the mad-house. These are exuberant exercises in rhetoric, full of paradoxes and historical fabrications, sweeping the reader along with a kind of facetious indifference to the standards of rational argument. Instead of argument Foucault sees 'discourse'; in the place of truth he sees power. In Foucault's view, all discourse gains acceptance by expressing, fortifying and concealing the power of those who maintain it; and those who, from time to time, perceive this fact are invariably imprisoned as criminals or locked away as mad – a fate that Foucault himself unaccountably avoided.

Foucault's approach reduces culture to a power game, and scholarship to a kind of refereeing in the endless 'struggle' between oppressed and oppressing groups. The shift of emphasis from the content of an utterance to the power that speaks through it leads to a new kind of scholarship, which bypasses entirely questions of truth and rationality, and can even reject those questions as themselves ideological.

The pragmatism of the late American philosopher Richard Rorty is of similar effect. It expressly set itself against the idea of objective truth, giving a variety of arguments for thinking that truth is a negotiable thing, that what matters in the end is which side you are on. If a doctrine is useful in the struggle that liberates your group, then you are entitled to dismiss the alternatives.

Whatever you think of Foucault and Rorty, there is no doubt that they were intelligent writers and genuine scholars with a distinctive vision of reality. They opened the way to fakes but were not fakes themselves. Matters are quite otherwise with many of their contemporaries. Consider the following sentence:

> This is not just its situation 'in principle' (the one it occupies in the hierarchy of instances in relation to the determinant instance: in society, the economy) nor just its situation 'in fact' (whether, in the phase under consideration, it is dominant or subordinate) but the relation of this situation in fact to this situation in principle, that is, the very relation which makes of this situation in fact a 'variation' of the – 'invariant' – structure, in dominance, of the totality.

Or this:

> it is the connexion between signifier and signifier that
> permits the elision in which the signifier installs the lack-of-
> being in the object relation using the value of 'reference back'
> possessed by signification in order to invest it with the desire
> aimed at the very lack it supports.

Those sentences are from the French philosopher Louis Althusser
and the French psychoanalyst Jacques Lacan respectively. These
authors emerged from the revolutionary ferment of Paris in
1968 to achieve an astonishing reputation, not least in America,
where between them they run up more references in the
academic literature than Kant and Goethe combined. Yet it is
surely clear that these sentences are nonsense. Their claims to
scholarship and erudite knowledge intimidate the critic and
maintain fortified defences against critical assault. They illustrate
a peculiar kind of academic Newspeak: each sentence is curled
round like an ingrowing toenail, hard, ugly and pointing only
to itself.

The fake intellectual invites you to conspire in his own self-
deception, to join in creating a fantasy world. He is the teacher
of genius, you the brilliant pupil. Faking is a social activity in
which people act together to draw a veil over unwanted realities
and encourage each other in the exercise of their illusory
powers. The arrival of fake thought and fake scholarship in our
universities should not therefore be attributed to any explicit
desire to deceive. It has come about through the complicit
opening of territory to the propagation of nonsense. Nonsense
of this kind is a bid to be accepted. It asks for the response: by
God, you are right, it is like that.

And no doubt if you have earned your academic career by
learning to push around the nonsensical mantras of the impostors,
combining them in the impenetrable syntax that hoodwinks the
person who composes it as much as the person who reads it, you
will react indignantly to everything I have said so far.

Indeed, it could be argued that the rise of fake scholarship and fake philosophy matters little. Such things can be contained within the university, which is their natural home, and make little difference to the lives of ordinary people. Yet when we think of high culture and its importance, we tend to think not of scholarship and philosophy but of art, literature and music – activities that are only accidentally connected to the university, and that influence the quality of life and the goals of people outside the academy.

There are consequences of fake culture that are comparable to the consequences of corruption in politics. In a world of fakes the public interest is constantly sacrificed to private fantasy, and the truths on which we depend for our rescue are left unexamined and unknown. But to prove the point is a hard task indeed, and after a lifetime of attempts I find myself only at the beginning.

PART NINE

Animal Rights, Pulpit Politics and Sex

Male Domination

(*The Times*, 1983)

What's wrong with rape? The question must naturally arise when women complain of the ease with which this crime has been committed and excused. Is rape like theft, a matter of taking without consent that which belongs to another? But then, what is taken? And what kind of 'belonging' is this, which ruins the life of the person who loses it and never enriches the thief?

Masculine thinking is dominated by the idea of contract. It sees legitimate society as an exchange of rights and promises and most crime as an attempt to cheat one's way to the common goal. For such an attitude the extremes of evil are incomprehensible, because indescribable. If it seems surprising to men that rape should carry a maximum penalty equal to that for murder, then this is because they have been misled into thinking that the sin of taking the short cut to another's private property differs only in degree from the sin of taking the short cut to her private parts.

But it is precisely because sex is a private matter that the feminine mind is better able to comprehend. A moment's reflection should persuade us of the woman's view, which is that the rapist, unlike the thief, does not so much deprive as annihilate his victim. He is indifferent to the other's consent, since he is indifferent to the other's existence. His rage is the rage of lust, which is fired by the sight of the human body but dismayed by the presence of the human soul. His victim is therefore forced to suffer an act that expressly severs her from her body, and which causes her to see her own body as alien. The rapist plunders not property but life itself. For it is only on the premise of an identity between soul and body that human life is liveable.

Feminists are surely right, therefore, when they see in the crime of rape vital proof of the male desire to negate the female. Rape is the extreme form of a pervasive masculine ambition, which is to replace sexual desire by the pursuit of the sexual commodity. Sexual desire is a longing to be united with another person, and tenderness (which is a frenzy of mutual consent) is the essence of its bond.

Desire has nothing to do with the urge to relieve oneself upon the body of another. To women this urge is loathsome in every way, and not the least because it allows the values of the market to pollute those of the hearth. Men, however, are wary of true desire, since tenderness imbues the sexual act with responsibilities. By vividly symbolizing the presence of another human soul, it hampers freedom and diminishes power. This is the true reason why men seek to debase women. The transformation of woman into a commodity raises excitement and diminishes desire. Hence it fulfils the long-term masculine ambition, which is to make women undesirable, and so to open the way to discarding them.

This ambition has achieved remarkable successes in recent years. It has used a variety of stratagems, of which three deserve mention. First, it has pulled about the myth that sexuality is a merely 'animal' function and the sexual act a kind of compulsive discharge, of no intrinsic moral significance; no matter how or with whom you do it, you are never really to blame. This myth has been inculcated by pseudo-scientific documents, such as the Kinsey report, and also by campaigns for sex education in schools. The initial aim has always been to replace important moral ideas such as modesty and shame (ideas without which sexual desire is inconceivable) with a tidy notion of 'sexual hygiene', which, by abolishing mystery, abolishes desire.

The second masculine stratagem is that of indecency, of which rape is merely the most fully realized and most violent form. In a persuasive analysis of pornography ('The Politics of Sex', *Salisbury Review*, no. 2) Robert Grant points to the damage inflicted on human sexuality by the market in indecent publications. Pornography, he writes, effectively authorizes lust by freeing it from moral scruple. It insulates the 'consumer' from the situation depicted. Because he participates in nothing, his excitement is freed from the obstructions of tenderness and his interest in another body need never be deflected by the awareness of another soul. Pornography is therefore the perfect preparation for a sexual ambition that aims to sever soul and body, so as to possess the second without paying the price exacted by the first.

But both of these stratagems are fraught with dangers. They are too conscious, too evident, too vulnerable to popular reaction. In a world where women may ascend to positions of influence they risk, in the long run, a strong impediment from the law: it is presumably only a normal preoccupation with inessentials that has caused our leaders to neglect this particular duty. Hence the third most powerful stratagem, which is to infiltrate the camp of the enemy, so as to make women speak against their own interests in their own voice.

This brilliant tactic, which bears all the marks of masculine perfidy, calls itself 'feminism', rather in the way the communist enslavement calls itself 'peace'. It propagates the extraordinary myth that the division of sexual roles, the institution of the family, the ideals of modesty and chastity are all male inventions, designed to confine women to a situation that thwarts their true development. In truth, of course, these are precisely the bonds from which men have always sought to free themselves.

By propagating feminist ideology, therefore, men hope to rid the sexual impulse of its debilitating commitment. No longer subject to the pangs of sexual desire, they may then begin to regulate their relations with women by the laws of the market-place, and so allow no claims of allegiance to extinguish the claims of power.

The Pestilence of Pulpit Politics

(*The Times*, 1983)

The National Conference of Roman Catholic Priests, which met recently in Birmingham, was attended by 93 clergymen. Since there are more than 5,000 Roman Catholic priests in England and Wales, it cannot be said with any certainty that the assembly was representative. Nevertheless it was vociferous, and the opinions of the vociferous count for much in this world, even if, as one may hope, they count for nothing in the next.

The increasing predominance of conferences in pastoral affairs is part of the process whereby the Roman Catholic Church has been transformed from a prescriptive authority, whose currency is faith, to a debating chamber, dealing in the inflationary coinage of opinion. It is inevitable that such a body should begin to turn away from what matters in religion, the eternal verities, towards what, *sub specie aeternitatis*, matters least of all – the affairs of this world, which can be the subject of opinion only because they lie outside the domain of faith.

The National Conference therefore followed in the footsteps of the National Pastoral Congress of 1980, and the Bishops' Conference of England and Wales, in devoting time and energy to secular causes. And Cardinal Basil Hume himself exhorted those present to involve themselves 'much more in the institutions of our land, in neighbourhood organizations, trade unions, local government and parliament'.

We must remember that a certain kind of politics is, for a priest, an easy way out. It is far more agreeable to exalt oneself through compassion for what is anonymous and abstract – the working class, the victims of capitalist oppression, the Third World – than to work humbly in the ways of charity, which obliges us to help those concrete, knowable and often unlovable individuals whom Providence has placed in our path.

Not only is it more agreeable, it is also more gratifying to the ego. The attention of the world is more readily captured by the man with a cause then by the man who merely attends to his duty. There lies the origin of the modern heresy, which sees true religion in large-scale worldly enterprises and which exhorts us to fight oppression in Chile, racism in South Africa or nuclear weapons at home – in short, to perfect the unfinished work of Providence – rather than to save our own souls. It is significant, indeed, that the causes chosen by those in the grip of this heresy are precisely those which further the interests of the world's most militant atheist power.

Addressing the National Conference, the chaplain to the University of East Anglia argued against the obligatory fast on Friday, on the ground that, because young people did not see the sense of it, this practice was an obstacle to his apostolic work. One would have thought that his duty was to *make* them see the sense of it. Besides, young people seem to be magnetized by those religions, however eccentric in doctrine or rococo in performance, which try to control their eating habits. But the chaplain's complaint eloquently captures the apostolic incompetence of a Church dedicated to secular affairs.

Man knows that he is not self-created, and he knows therefore that he owes a debt of gratitude, which can be repaid only by obedience. But obedience to what? Until he answers that question, he lives in a state of anxiety; it is the central tenet of Christian doctrine that the answer lies in faith. With faith a man may at last do with an easy heart what he otherwise does only hesitantly: he may fast and pray. Someone who does not see the sense of such activities is someone who is not yet in a position to believe. Someone who does see the sense of them sees also that they are performed not only for the sake of others but also, and principally, for the sake of oneself, that one may be reconciled with the power to whom one's life is owed.

The strength of the traditional Roman Catholic Church was twofold. It offered a definite and authoritative system of answers to life's questions, worked out over centuries of discussion and inquiry and delivered in a language that spoke directly to the individual heart. It also rehearsed, in sublime ritual, the mystery of man's condition and the universality of the Church which promised his redemption. This certainty and self-containment were the grounds of its success. For no convert can be won by a religion that compromises with his doubts and hesitations, or which puts secular causes in the place of individual salvation.

No doubt the majority of priests realize that. No doubt they accept that their duty lies towards the individual sinner, for whose sake they must renounce so many of life's pleasures – including the pleasure of trumpeting abroad their virtuous concern for peace and social justice. The true priest works quietly, outside the publicity that gravitates to those of little faith.

The oral instructions offered to his flock by one such priest – Monsignor Alfred Gilbey – have recently been recorded and transcribed by a group of his friends. *We Believe* is a remarkable document, written with warm emotion and lucid intellect. It completely demolishes the secular superstitions with which the faith of Rome has recently been confounded, and presents a doctrine sufficiently complete and sufficiently rich in implications for the individual life as to make conversion possible. It does, indeed, what all apostolic writing must do, and what so much modern Catholic literature refrains from doing: it presents belief to the unbeliever. My thought on closing the book was: if this were true, as it is beautiful, then it would suffice.

On the Eating of Fish

(*The Times*, 1984)

Increasingly, Englishmen spend the summer not at the seaside but in the country. For pastoral sentiment forms the rhetoric of urban life, and the person whose daily horizon consists of walls and chimneys imagines a countryside beyond them, into which he will soon be released, free from man-made squalor and man-made anxiety.

Pastoral sentiments are to be resisted, with the same fervour as pacifism, vegetarianism and wholemeal bread. For they encourage us to forget the truth, which is that nature too is man-made. Some say (though they are a scholarly minority) that it was made by Theocritus and Virgil. Others blame nature on the Dutch landscape painters, others still on the Augustan poets. Personally, I hold the farmers responsible. It is they who manage this expensive tapestry. In particular, they support the animals, which provide the main visual delight in any country scene. With their discreet munching and rustling, animals transform the inert cloth of green into a cloak of living movement.

The cows, sheep, hens and horses owe their comfortable existence to man. So too do wilder and more colourful things. Pheasants, partridges, ducks and hares all take their lives from the men who kill them, and who take trouble so that they might survive. Vegetarians and other animal-haters detest this symbiotic harmony. But they should remember that the hunter threatens only the individual creature in his sights, while they threaten the species.

Food has become a moral issue. We are told repeatedly that everything we eat is bad for us. Such speculations are impious and selfish. Life too is bad for us, and if we wish to live well, we should live for others. Eat, therefore, that others may live. Eat animals – as many animals as you possibly can – so as to fulfil your duty to the great chain of being.

But this brings me to a problem that has yet to be properly solved: the problem of fish. Those Englishmen who still spend their holidays by the seaside do not take pleasure in the life beneath the waves. Indeed, their enjoyment would be greater if the sea were dead. Realizing this, they eat not fish and chips but fried chicken, hoping that the vast quantities of fish meal on which the battery hens are fed will make a greater inroad into the remaining maritime fauna. Killing fish would of course be a help to fish, if only we could increase their chances of survival. But we cannot, so that this turning away from fish and chips towards fried chicken offers a threat not only to our last remaining national tradition but also to the life of the sea.

Or so I used to think. I therefore drew the conclusion that eating fish is wrong. And I had the support of British fishmongers everywhere, whose stalls bear witness to a distinct lack of enthusiasm for anything that emerges from the water. Bland white tablets divorced from their anatomical meaning, headless flakes of muscle, yellow fishcakes, oily brown kippers looking like a pair of dustman's gloves – such sights testify to a profound loathing for the life of the deep and a desire to return all scaly, slimy things to the place whence they came.

But the problem is not so easily solved. There is another reason for eating, besides the fact that it gives support to nature's lower orders. Wine cannot stand alone: it needs food as its moral foundation. Fish is the only possible accompaniment to white burgundy, and fish must therefore be eaten if white burgundy is to be drunk. Not any fish, however: not the denatured artefact of the English fish stall but fish in all its natural horrendousness, with grinning jaws, bulging eyes and the full carnival of colours that plays such an inexplicable role in the fashions of the deep.

Overeating these creatures does not ensure their survival. But the human species justifies its existence by its inventive powers. We may soon discover ways of helping the John Dory, the grey mullet, the hake and the scallop, as we have helped the partridge and the hare. We will have the motive, however, only if we continue to eat fish. Perhaps, therefore, eating fish is as much a duty as eating animals. For those who appreciate white burgundy, it may also be a pleasure.

That last remark is slightly contentious. I conclude, therefore, with a recipe for a dish that provides the perfect accompaniment to a fine old Meursault. Take two heads of hake. (The fishmonger will have thrown the vile things into the waste bucket.) Turn them into a stock, using fennel, onion, celery, lemon juice and Chablis. In the strained stock you must then simmer (for no more than five minutes) six scallops and 2 lb. of monkfish. Since monkfish generates a lot of water, leave it to drain into the stock. Then reduce the liquid, thicken it with a white roux, add six capers, some green peppercorns, salt, fresh basil and double cream. Cut the fish into mouth-sized pieces, cover with the sauce (which must be as thick as treacle) and bake for the least possible time in a pie, made with short pastry into which you have incorporated a quantity of flaked almonds. Fortunately, children hate this dish; it will therefore be enough for the whole family.

Obligations of the Flesh

(*The Times*, 1985)

Surrogate motherhood should be seen in its wider context: not as an answer to the problems of sterility but as the outcome of a revision in moral perceptions comparable to that foretold in *Brave New World*. The citizens of Huxley's earthly paradise have a horror of motherhood, and attach to the process of childbirth the shame and the sense of contamination that our ancestors attached to sexual union. At the same time, the sexual act itself is without danger to them – a hygienic exercise, no more problematic than the brushing of teeth and rather more pleasurable.

The idea that sexual union is to be understood in terms of its generative tendency is foreign to their perceptions, since it implies that the human body might harbour a destiny and a responsibility greater than any that can be imposed by the all-powerful, impersonal and all-absolving State. It is for the abstract machinery of government to decide who shall exist, to take responsibility for his manufacture and to circumscribe his life. The sexual organs have no function other than fleeting pleasure, and to associate them with the crippling liabilities of childbirth, or the compromising destiny of a warm physical love, is to commit a terrible obscenity.

Naturally we have not yet advanced so far. Nevertheless, certain elements of Huxley's vision have been realized. Contraception has effectively severed the sexual act from its generative tendency, and, as Germaine Greer has argued, pregnancy now appears like a misfortune, or even a disease. Moreover, a scientific view of the human embryo has revised our idea of motherhood. As well a test-tube as a womb. And what matters that it should be this womb rather than that? Why not a womb detached from the human body, and preserved in laboratory conditions as a producer of children?

The unborn child is no longer a human person, attached by indelible rights and obligations to the mother who bears him, but a slowly ripening deformity, which can be aborted at will, should the mother choose to cure herself. In surrogate motherhood the relation between mother and child ceases to issue from the very body of the mother and is severed from the experience of incarnation. The bond between mother and child is demystified, made clear, intelligible, scientific – and also provisional, revocable and of no more than contractual force.

We should not see this as an isolated result of scientific progress. In just the same way the sexual bond has become clear and intelligible, and also provisional, revocable and of merely contractual force, governed by the morality of adult 'consent'. We have suffered a universal demystification of the human body. It has ceased to be the sacred fount of our deepest obligations and become instead a mere organism, obedient to the biological imperatives that govern all living things. Because we know ourselves in another way, however – as free beings, bound by a moral law – we begin to doubt the moral prerogative of the body. It no longer seems possible to us that the merely *bodily* character of our acts can determine their moral value. Hence arises the extraordinary view that the homosexual act, considered in itself, is morally indistinguishable from the heterosexual act: for what is there, in its merely physical character, to justify the traditional stigma?

The liberal morality which tells us to permit the body's pleasures and to stifle the impulse of shame expresses, in effect, a peculiar metaphysical vision of the body as somehow detached from the self and outside the sphere of our true obligations. To the liberated conscience it seems absurd that the prophet of Islam, enjoining us to charitable behaviour, should add that we must conceal our private parts. What a ludicrous mixture of moral truth and childlike superstition! And yet, in this as in many things, Muhammad's instinct was sure. We are not separate from our bodies but identical with them, and inculpated not only by our actions but also by our pleasures and postures and by bodily exposure to our kind.

Traditional sexual morality was an instrument whereby people came to terms with their incarnation and took moral responsibility for their flesh. The two earthly loves that prompt and fulfil our existence — sexual love and the love of children — issue from the body by a process that we may see in neutral, scientific terms only at our peril. For these are forces by which we live and which govern our smaller obligations. To regard the process that generates them as subject to revision and revocation is to set the body outside the sphere of moral sentiment and to cease to take responsibility for one's flesh. It is to exchange the moral security of corporal existence for a fantasy of ultimate freedom, in which all our obligations are of our own devising and the tyrant destiny is overcome. But there cannot be such an ultimate freedom, and all that is achieved by our constant striving towards it is the slow alienation from our bodily condition and the gradual poisoning of the carnal source of love.

In such matters, St Augustine argued, the body appears to have a will of its own, and its constant disobedience, he added, is the testimony to original sin. But if original sin resides in the body, it is because we reside there too. Hence we should never lose sight of the fundamental truth that some uses of the body are sinful, and none more so than those which enable us to escape the obligations that the body itself imposes.

Eat Animals! It's for Their Own Good

(*Los Angeles Times*, 1991)

Animals, like people, can be nice or nasty. Nice animals do not bite or kick; you can stroke them, gurgle at them and ride them; they even become adept at simulating human affection, enabling unloved people to experience fantasies of love.

Nasty animals do not bite and kick continuously. They often brood about their captive state until the day comes for revenge. The pit bull terrier, for instance, will behave impeccably for years before suddenly killing his keeper, an outcome that may be welcomed by everyone else. Unfortunately he will usually try to kill everyone else as well.

How should we deal with nasty animals? The British Parliament has decided that certain breeds of dog – the pit bull being one – should be either shot or neutered. This has led to protests from the owners, many of whom worked long and hard to obtain a pet whose temperament matched their own. Some pit bull owners, notwithstanding their contempt for the human species, have even decided to vote Socialist in the next election. Meanwhile, the Labour Party has included 'animal rights' in its electoral programme, following its policy of looking for support among freaks and fanatics, in the hope that, after 20 years of Socialist education policy, freaks and fanatics now outnumber men of common sense.

Add to the question of dangerous dogs those of hunting, whaling, zoos, vivisection, factory farming, pest control and the ecosphere, and you will see that henceforth animals are going to be high on the political agenda. It is therefore time to lay down some principles for dealing with them.

First principle: Animals have no rights. Humans have rights because we are rational beings, who exist by negotiation and by the reciprocal recognition of duties. A creature that cannot recognize the rights of others cannot claim rights for itself. Only if animals had duties, therefore, would they also have rights. But it would then be wrong to capture them, kill them, eat them, to keep them as pets, to train them to stand on their hind legs or to make use of them in any way.

A dog has neither rights nor duties, but his owner has both. Don't punish the dog, therefore, but the owner. Make him liable by law for the damage done by his pet; the cost of insuring a pit bull will then rapidly lead to the extinction of the breed.

Second principle: We are now stewards of the animal kingdom. Henceforth no species exists without our permission. We therefore have some difficult choices to make. Favour shown to the chicken is bad news for the fox, while our liking for horses and cows has virtually abolished the lion.

Third principle: We can provide for the animals only if we have a sufficient motive. And 'we' does not mean pampered intellectuals but rural primitives, rednecks and the kind of person who would like to keep a pit bull. Fortunately, the motive exists. There is no better way of protecting the habitat of a species than by systematically hunting it. It is angling that has saved England's rivers from pollution, stag-hunting that has preserved our native deer, fox-hunting that has saved our hedgerows and shooting that has filled our meadows with pheasant and our moors with grouse. Similarly, it is big-game hunting that will save the safari parks of Africa and whaling that will save the whale. Elephants may be threatened by ivory poachers, but not so much as they would benefit from ivory farmers, who would have an interest in protecting them. As it is, however, the short-sighted ban on the trade in ivory will probably lead to the extinction of the elephant.

Fourth principle: Animals that we eat have the best chance of competing for space on our planet. We therefore have a duty to eat meat – as much meat and in as many varieties as possible. Every vegetarian meal is a crime against nature.

This does not mean that we can treat animals as we will. We should give them a chance to run around, copulate, bark, neigh and roar as the spirit moves them. And when the time comes, we should choose a lenient form of death – shooting, say, or hunting with hounds, rather than the trapping and poisoning that have cast such shame on the human race. One last plea for mercy, therefore: let us reintroduce the rat-catching terrier, which is the true friend of the rat. A rat hunt, culminating in a swift biting-off of the offending head, is much to be preferred to the slow agonies of poisoning; it is also ecologically cleaner, provides healthy entertainment for all the family and encourages sympathy for the rat – one of nature's most unjustly despised and affectionate creatures.

Sextants and Sexting

(previously unpublished, 2009)

Human beings are wanderers, who roam the world in search of adventure. And this love of adventure creates a need for home: homecoming makes wandering worthwhile.

Hence human beings have devised instruments that help them to navigate, so as to guide them to their destination and – most importantly – to guide them back again, to the place where they are at home.

The sextant was one of the most beautiful examples of this: an instrument for steering by the stars, which you held to your eye, and which reminded you of the vastness of the space across which you peered and the littleness of your own ambitions. Our ancestors who steered by the sextant never doubted the fixed background to human life, the unchanging heavens by which they navigated. There was a place they were going but also a place where they belonged. Adventures ended in homecoming, and the need for home remained. Thanks to the sextant they could venture further and still return safely; but it was they, and not the sextant, that chose where to go.

Modern gadgets are not like that. They are less and less our servants and more and more our masters. We think we can use them to achieve our ends, only to discover that they are using us to achieve ends that we had never anticipated and which nobody owns. The adventures to which they tempt us are far easier to embark on than those journeys of our ancestors across the seas. And they seem to be entirely without danger.

We travel round the world with the click of a mouse; we visit friends and strangers on the screen, chat on the mobile phone and post on our Facebook wall all the things we want the world to know. We can sit at our desk and enjoy every kind of thrill at no cost in danger. So we think. But all the while the World Wide Web is reaching out to us, and we are caught like flies, wriggling in the suffocating bonds of screen addiction. And it is only then that we realize that we don't know the way back; that we are sitting at our desk but far, far indeed from home.

The power of gadgets to enter and possess the human soul is brought out by the new vice of sexting. What an adventure, to take a picture of yourself all naked, and send it to your boyfriend of the moment. The mobile phone is there, asking you to do it. And what's the problem, when nobody sees? Thus it is that girls have fallen into the latest trap, only to discover their nude image in the mobile phones of friends and enemies, in the fantasies of strangers, in the lustful plans of predating men and displayed all over cyberspace.

How to get back home from this one? We should not be surprised that one girl, unable to live with her prostituted image, has committed suicide, and that others are finding themselves in trouble with parents, teachers and the law.

The problem is not the use to which the gadget has been put, but the gadget itself. Sextants were innocent means to our ends which had no agenda of their own. Modern gadgets are not like that. They are bundles of temptation. They offer new choices, new visions, new adventures. They stand at the door of your life, asking to take over. And young people, who have no defences against them, very quickly invite them in.

Parents like to think that, by providing their child with a mobile phone, they are providing him or her with a mere instrument, something that can be used for legitimate purposes that already exist – like letting your parents know where you are and when to collect you. In fact they are providing their child with a new master, one designed by sophisticated adults to take over the person in whose hand it sits.

Unfortunately, because of television and the internet, people have lost the sense that images are morally questionable. All images are OK, provided they are in the hands for which they were intended. The Old Testament and Koranic interdiction against 'graven images' extended to the human form, and in all cultures people have looked warily on images that are sexually explicit. This wariness is now disappearing, and the first victims are children – those who are just beginning to be aware of themselves as sexual subjects and don't yet know the cost of being a sexual object instead.

A culture of resistance among parents could help, of course. There are those who refuse to have televisions because of the rubbish that pours from them. And there are those who train their children to survive without a mobile phone, as until recently everybody did. There are those who allow the mobile phone but not in the bedroom. And so on. But still the problem remains for the majority of teenagers, who are left to their own devices, which turn out to be the vices of their devices.

There is only one clear way forward, which is to recognize that the shame that young people, and girls in particular, used to feel at being seen naked is not itself shameful – that, on the contrary, shame is, as Scheler said, a *Schutzgefühl*, a protective feeling, which is part of healthy sexual development. To teach this to children today, when the whole tendency of their courses in 'sex education' and 'health education' is in the opposite direction, will be hard. But maybe one good consequence of sexting will be in persuading parents and teachers that there is no other remedy.

Tally Ho! Let the Hunt Remind Us of Who We Are

(Daily Telegraph, 2012)

This morning hundreds of hunts across the kingdom will be assembling for the Boxing Day meet. My family and I will appear in our polished uniforms on polished horses to stand ceremonially among our neighbours in Cirencester Park. With us will be a crowd of thousands who have come to enjoy the spectacle. For an hour three species – hound, horse and human; carnivore, herbivore and omnivore – will stand peacefully side by side in a little patch of meadowland, radiating tranquillity. One of the local bands will be playing. The Royal Agricultural College Beagles will be there, along with people from every walk of life, who have come to gladden their eyes on the spectacle before going for lunch in the town.

Hunting with hounds is ostensibly a crime. It continues, not because hunting people wish to defy the law, but because an activity so central to their lives can no more be stopped than their heartbeats. They have had to adjust. But they cannot live in the countryside without also sharing it with their animals.

I first encountered hunting in my early 40s. It was quite by chance that I should be trotting down a Cotswold lane on a friend's old pony when the uniformed centaurs came galloping past. One minute I was lost in solitary thoughts, the next I was in a world transfigured by collective energy. Imagine opening your front door one morning to put out the milk bottles and finding yourself in a vast cathedral in ancient Byzantium, the voices of the choir resounding in the dome above you and the congregation gorgeous in their holiday robes. My experience was comparable. The energy that swept me away was neither human nor canine nor equine but a peculiar synthesis of the three: a tribute to centuries of mutual dependence, revived for this moment in ritual form.

There is a singular and indescribable joy that comes from the co-operation between species. We go out together, a tribe, a herd and a pack, and move together in mutual understanding. We share dangers and triumphs, we are exhilarated and downcast simultaneously, and there grows between us a kind of unsentimental attachment that is stronger and deeper than any day-to-day companionship. This experience has been celebrated since ancient times. From the boar hunt that begins at line 428 of Homer's *Odyssey* to the fox hunt that forms the climax of Trollope's *The Eustace Diamonds*, hunting has been used to lift characters from their daily circumstances and to place them in another predicament, which rouses their animal spirits and puts them to a very special kind of test. The wall of domesticity has been broken down and we cross it to 'the other side of Eden', as the anthropologist Hugh Brody describes the world of the hunter–gatherer.

In that world animals are not the tamed and subservient creatures of the farmyard or the family house; they are our equals, with whom we are joined in a contest that may prove as dangerous to the hunter as it is to his quarry. In the paintings that adorn the caves of Lascaux we see the beasts of the wilderness portrayed by people who lived in awe of them, who conjured them into their own human dwelling place. The aura that emanates from these images emanates also from our hunting literature, reminding us that we too are animals and that we live with an unpaid debt towards the creatures from whom we have stolen the Earth.

In a sense we know much about the experience of the hunter–gatherer, since it is the experience that shaped us, and which lies interred like an archaeological stratum beneath the polished consciousness of civilized man. At its greatest, the art and literature of hunting aims to retrieve that experience, to reacquaint us with mysterious and sacred things which are the true balm to our suburban anxieties, but which can be recuperated now only by returning, in imagination, to a world that we have lost.

In hunting you are following, and the thing you follow is a pack of hounds, which in turn follows a scent. Some follow on horseback and are part of the action; others follow on foot, or by bicycle or car. All are returning, to a certain extent, to a pre-agrarian condition. The landscape is being 'thrown open' to its pre-historical use, and although the freedom taken by the hunt is at the same time a freedom offered by those with the power to forbid it, both parties to the deal are recapturing freedom of another and more deeply implanted kind. Hunting, which dissolves the boundaries between species, dissolves the boundaries between people too.

The thrill of jumping comes from this: you are abolishing the boundary that had vainly tried to exclude you. For a brief moment you are laying aside the demands of farming, and the man-centred individualism that farming engenders, and roaming across a landscape that has not yet been parcelled out and owned. The fields that I see from my window do not, for me, end at my boundary but stretch beyond it, to the place where the hounds of the Vale of White Horse hunt must be called off from the territory of the Old Berkshire, where 'ours' becomes 'theirs' and the riot of followers must turn back.

That feeling of 'ours' is expressed in many social events besides hunting: in fun rides, farmers' breakfasts, hunt balls and point-to-points. Those events form part of an intricate web of social relations through which we join in the collective possession of our whole locality and override our separate private claims. It is this sense of community that will bring us all together today, in order to renew our commitment to the place where we are.

PART TEN

Annus Horribilis and Last Words

Diary

(*Spectator*, 17 April 2019)

I travel back from London with the *St Matthew Passion* filling my head, after the moving performance from the Elysian Singers and Royal Orchestral Society under Sam Laughton at St James's, Piccadilly. Why does that last chord send shivers down the spine? The dark instrumentation, the sense that it is not an ending but a beginning, that this shadow-filled saraband will repeat itself for ever? Or is it just the story – surely one of the greatest narratives in all literature, in which nothing is redundant and yet everything is said? I arrive home with the chord still in my head, C minor with a B natural thrust like a sword into its heart. It foretells the week ahead. I devote the rest of the day to my report for the Building Better, Building Beautiful Commission.

*   *   *

The commission has concluded that beauty in ordinary architecture is inseparable from the sense of place. I explain it to the family. It is almost the first time we have sat down to dinner since work started on the commission some three months ago. What a relief it will be when it is over at last, and we can be together in the place that is ours.

*   *   *

On Tuesday, at a meeting of the commissioners and advisory board, I explain our work so far: visits, conversations, focus groups and the public spirit and decency of all the people we have encountered. Even if the politicians are at a loss to understand the problem, the people seem clear about it. The problem is ugliness – the glass and concrete cubes in the towns, the houses dumped in the fields without streets, centres or public spaces, the abuse of historic settlements and cherished landscapes that once were somewhere and now are nowhere. Do we have a solution? I am determined to find one.

* * *

To Paris on the Eurostar – always a treat, not least because it leaves from St Pancras, the clearest proof that beauty, utility, popularity and adaptability all go together. Something similar greets you in the Gare du Nord, though here it is the façade and the street that generate the sense of place. I am met by Damien Seyrinx, my publisher, and we go straight to the 16ème, where I am to discuss the French translation of *Fools, Frauds and Firebrands: Thinkers of the New Left* on France Culture. Unlike the BBC, the radio palace is sparsely frequented, with isolated figures working in boxes, some of them reading books. The interviewer is polite, and I am looked on with gentle compassion before being dispatched back to a peculiar country that cannot make up its mind about anything but which nevertheless is still admired, not least because it can produce something so weird as a conservative philosopher. I am pressed for time and Damien orders a taxi moto, which speeds me to the Gare du Nord in 20 minutes of hair-raising architectural glimpses. I telephone home, to learn that I have been sacked from my position as chair of the Building Better, Building Beautiful Commission. It was bound to happen, but I am astonished to learn that it is because the slanderous stories about me are all being recycled. How did this come about? I must have given an interview somewhere! And then I recall a slimy whippersnapper from the *New Statesman* who came to visit, saying the paper wished to write about my books.

* * *

Miraculously my family forgive me for that interview. The children are adamant that there should be no resentment but even a measure of sympathy towards the journalist. He probably thought that you make friends on the left by making enemies on the right. I open the computer: hundreds of emails in support, but nothing official to say what I have done wrong. If there is evidence to incriminate me, then obviously the *New Statesman* must make the tapes of the conversation public: how else will any of us know what we are allowed and not allowed to say, when working for this government?

* * *

I am more cheerful on Friday. Emails arrive from friends in Poland, Slovakia, Hungary, Czech Republic, Latvia, Slovenia and the US, all saying that they had once believed in British conservatism but can do so no longer. My favourite rabbi from Jerusalem offers to rally 'Jews for Scruton'; my favourite architect from Homs quotes consoling verses from the Koran; my favourite journalist on *Le Figaro* says we'll come out fighting. The family is right: don't feel resentment, but be grateful instead. If this hadn't happened, I would not have known the weight of friendship behind me.

* * *

The week ends with a trip to Cambridge for the memorial celebration for one of the dearest of my friends, the mathematician, biologist and musician Graeme Mitchison, who died of a brain tumour last year. He would have understood exactly what Bach meant by that C minor chord with a hole in it.

After My Own Dark Night

(*Daily Telegraph*, 2019)

Fully to understand the Easter story it helps to be hounded by the mob, to know that nothing that you say or do can deflect the hostility, and that in any case the distinctions between true and false, just and unjust, good and evil, have all been suspended. Some can undergo this experience in a spirit of charity, and one in particular rose above his suffering to forgive those who inflicted it.

The Easter story tells us of the redemption that comes into the world, when such torment is willingly undergone for others' sake. But it also tells us of the time of utter darkness, the time of nothingness, when the light of creation has gone out. St John of the Cross called this the dark night of the soul. The world lay in such a darkness on the first Easter Saturday; and at the end of this most terrible week a similar darkness fell on me.

Reading the outrageous articles in the *New Statesman*, *The Times*, the *Sun* and elsewhere, in which things that I have never said and attitudes that I have never entertained are unscrupulously pinned on me, seeing all my work as a writer and philosopher scribbled over with ignorant and groundless accusations, I have had to take stock of my life, and for a moment it seemed that it amounted to nothing. It was as though I had been ceremonially stripped of all my assets and shut away in a box.

This has happened before, but never with such an orchestrated clamour for my destruction. Dismissed without explanation from my government position, it seemed that I was even unwanted by the Conservative Party, to which I have offered a lifetime of intellectual support.

Philosophy is the pursuit of truth, and this has been, for me, a source of consolation in a difficult life. But in the real emergencies truth is not enough: we stand in need of examples, and of the stories that make suffering bearable, by showing that without it there is no redemption. Hence, in times of darkness, we turn to religion, in which another kind of truth is given to us. Experiences like the one that I have just undergone, however ordinary and human, have a part in the Easter story, and it is the genius of the Christian faith to make such easy room for them.

The root sentiment of Christianity is not triumph but defeat. It takes what is worst in human nature – the hounding of outsiders, the delight in cruelty, the betrayal of friends and the hatred of strangers – and winds these things into the story of Christ's passion. You too, it tells us, are members of this hate-filled mob. But you too can turn your hate to pity and your pity to love. That is what redemption means. That, to my mind, is the way to understand Easter Saturday. The world lies fragmented at the foot of the cross, as though un-created. We are shown the opposite of creation, a place of desolation where the light does not shine.

According to the old Christian story, Christ spent this day in the underworld, harrowing Hell. But we can understand the Easter message without that particular metaphor. In all of us there is a creative and outgoing principle – a principle of love, through which we renew our attachments and make a gift of our lives. When we cease to love, we are as though hollowed out, deprived of the force that sustains us in being. We become a void, a negation, a thing that should not be. And into the void flows the mob, eager for victims and ardent to destroy. That psychic mechanism is present in all of us. In the world of today, however, its effect is amplified. Twitter has made morons of us all, sweeping us along in a storm of rumour and spite. But Christians, contemplating the crucifixion, can still switch sides from the triumphant mob to the defeated victim. Through the bleakness of Easter Saturday they can experience the true meaning of the Cross, as the dark negative ushers in the Resurrection, and the light once again shines.

Indeed, the habit of focusing on the defeated victim, rather than the triumphant mob, is Christianity's strength. In the face of destruction the Christian opts for renewal. As Notre-Dame burned, the crowd of agnostics in the street below recovered for a moment their Christian faith, looking up to the Angel of the Resurrection, who stands as though shivering above the roof far above. As the angel promises, Notre-Dame will be reborn. Despite all that has happened to weaken Christianity in France, the Christian spirit remains, embodied in this cathedral dedicated to the protector of Paris, where she is prayed to by few but loved by many.

The Easter Saturday encounter with nothingness is a demonstration that the world must be constantly re-created. For many would-be Christians, however, the resurrection is a sticking point. Christ's death makes sense only on the assumption that he survived it; else he is simply one more in the endless stream of victims. Yet how can we believe in such an event, which so completely defies the laws of nature and for which we have only the sketchy evidence summarized in the Gospels, in the Acts of the Apostles and in the letters of St Paul? Leaving aside all learned theology, but taking inspiration from the poets, painters and composers who have treated this subject, I would say that Christ's resurrection, like his death, is an event in eternity. It occurs in me and in you, just so long as we put our trust in the possibility of renewal. It is a reaffirmation of the creative principle, and of the love that brought about Christ's death. The darkness that came over the world on that first Easter Saturday could be dispelled only by a renewal of this love, and this renewal comes through us. The cross is a display of supreme forgiveness, which invites us to forgive in our turn.

Seeing the Christian mystery in that way, we open a path to reconciliation with the other Abrahamic faiths. Christ's death is not a one-off event in ordinary time but, to borrow T. S. Eliot's words, 'the point of intersection of the timeless with time'. The wonderful concretion of the Gospels, which give us the shape and feel of Christ's earthly life, show love shining from a source beyond those vivid moments. To translate that idea into theological terms is not necessary. It is enough to see that there is a love that overcomes all suffering, all resentment, all negativity, and that this love is the source of our own renewal.

Which returns me to my ordeal. No sooner had the smears been published than I was inundated with messages of friendship and support. The life that I assumed to be over was now being renewed. I had undergone a death and a resurrection, and the gift of Easter had been laid on me even before I had asked for it.

My 2019

(*Spectator*, 21 December 2019)

January

My 2018 ended with a hate storm, in response to my appointment as chair of the government's Building Better, Building Beautiful Commission. But the new year brings a lull, and I hope and pray that the Grand Inquisitor enthroned by social media will find another target.

February

The 27th is my 75th birthday and, as it happens, the last Wednesday meet of foxhounds for the season. We host the meet and celebrate with our neighbours. Despite my wife Sophie's protests, I maintain my resolve to give up hunting at 75, counting again the broken bones, sprains and muscular disorders acquired over 35 years in the saddle, or rather, out of it. On my last hunt, I am glad to say, I stay in the saddle all day.

I try out my thoughts on *Parsifal* before a crowded meeting of the Wagner Society. Through a wonderful artistic contrivance Wagner connects redemption and suffering, showing that our highest aspirations grow from our darkest griefs, and that the gate to fulfilment stands on the way of loss. The music says this, even if the words and the plot shroud it in mystery. One member of the audience asks a penetrating question. I forget the question but remember the man, since five months later he is to save my life.

March

I have been dismayed to discover how many meetings, reports, visits and discussions are involved in a government commission. Creative writing is clearly impossible. My little book of stories, *Souls in the Twilight*, may have to stand in for all the other things I have wanted to write in my retirement. My agent suggests a relaunch in April. I go along with the idea, not anticipating what awaits me.

High points include a visit to Newcastle and Tynemouth, much-loved places where I could certainly live, notwithstanding the vandalization of the city in the '60s by councillors who treated collective responsibilities as personal gifts.

A visit to my dear friend Jonathan Ruffer at Bishop Auckland shows that our country also produces people who treat personal gifts as collective responsibilities. Jonathan convinces me that the regeneration of the north-east could be easily achieved if influential people were to see it the way he does, as a patriotic duty to be accomplished through faith.

April

My publisher, Bloomsbury, has agreed to an interview in the *New Statesman*, a magazine for which I retain a certain fondness, having served as its wine critic for several years. Unfortunately, Bloomsbury's publicity officer cannot make it to the interview, and I am alone with an eager young man who has come not to learn about my views but to reinforce his own. I think nothing of it, since the presence of a young and inquiring mind switches me to teacher mode, assuming knowledge in order to induce it. The fact that this person may be not just ignorant of the issues that crop up but interested only in the ways they can be used to damage me does not cross my mind.

Readers of *The Spectator* do not need reminding of the sequel. The interview is duly published – a mendacious concoction of out-of-context remarks and downright fabrications. We are able to obtain the tapes of the interview, and on the strength of this, and thanks to all the support that is offered to me, not least by this magazine and its brave associate editor Douglas Murray, I obtain an apology from the *New Statesman*.

By that time the damage has been done. I have been dismissed from the Commission, by a party that seems entirely unacquainted with the many thousands of quite well-argued words that I have offered in support of it, and the architects queue up to pour their ritual denunciations on my head.

At my lowest point, fearing that all the work conducted by the Commission would be lost, I communicate to James Brokenshire, Secretary of State for Housing, Communities and Local Government, that he should stick with it, and to his credit he does. It has been a hard time for Mr Brokenshire, but his apology leads to my reinstatement, and even the architectural press, apart from the adolescent *Dezeen*, ceases to repeat the fantastic and fabricated charges against me.

What lessons do I draw from this episode, apart from the obvious one that conservative intellectuals are being censored out of the public debate in our country? A headline in *The Times* informing the reader that I have been dismissed from a government position 'over "white supremacist" views'; an attack in parliament demanding that I be stripped of my knighthood in the light of my 'Islamophobic, anti-Semitic and homophobic comments' – and so on and so forth – such things naturally jeopardize my loyalty to the country and the party to which I have devoted so much of my energy over 50 years. 'Do I belong here?' I ask. To discover that even prominent members of the Tory party are inclined to say 'no' is a fairly shattering blow. But there is a good side. Letters of support come in from across the world, and for a while it is as though I am listening to the speeches at my own funeral, with the unique chance of nodding in agreement. And just in case I do think of emigrating, *Le Figaro* mounts a campaign in support of me, preparing the way.

But this reminds me of the real disaster in April. Writing in *Le Figaro* in the wake of the Notre-Dame fire, I pay my tribute to a city whose art and literature have been a continual inspiration since my first visit as a teenager. 'As the angel on the roof has promised,' I write,

> Notre-Dame will be resurrected. It will be resurrected because its city, unique among modern capitals, has remained continually itself, from the time when it was the heart of Europe, through the time when it turned the world upside down, to our present time, when it reminds our troubled continent of the spiritual inheritance that it must not deny.

Is that a pious hope or will the postmodern worldview of Emmanuel Macron still allow Europe to be what it really means to us? This question has animated politics across our continent throughout the year, and yet few people seem to be aware of it.

May

Sophie has arranged a belated birthday party with my closest friends. There are speeches to warm the heart, and a performance of my three settings of Lorca, sung by Emily Van Evera. David Matthews has composed a set of variations for violin and piano on 'Despedida' ('Farewell'), the last of the songs, and this melody which means so much to me stays in my head through the ensuing months, pointing in a direction that I soon discover to be the inevitable one.

June

I am in Poland to open the inter-parliamentary conference celebrating the first semi-free parliament in the former Soviet bloc, 30 years ago. All the countries that suffered are represented, and my task is to unite them around their original bid for freedom, downplaying the differences that have since grown between them. Many of the martyrs are there – old people recalling the 20- and 30-year prison sentences that were then the lot of those who think like me. Their moving testimonies leave me in a shocked and sober frame of mind, knowing how little all of this means to young British people today, as the knowledge of the history and culture of Europe slips from their grasp. Because I have taken their experiences seriously over the years, the Poles consider me entitled to their Order of Merit, duly conferred by the President. With an added touch of Polish humour they also confer the Ministry of Culture's prize for architecture. Needless to say, the British ambassador is absent from these embarrassing events, and I escape to England with a heart full of gratitude for another country where I would be welcome as a refugee.

July

And it is not the only one. For reasons I do not truly fathom I have a fan club in Brazil, and have finally agreed to turn up there to talk about the meaning of life. I am not feeling well, and the journey puts a strain on me. I stay in my hotel, reading Shakespeare. I groan in discomfort above streets where no sane man would walk, and am carted around to give lectures to crowds of young people, all of whom seem to be devoted to the task of saving Western civilization in the furthest point it has reached, which turns out to be Brazil. Maybe they are better able than I am to see the alternative is not another and better civilization, but no civilization at all.

Returning to London, I finally get to see the rheumatologist with whom I have booked an appointment. He talks of my lecture on *Parsifal*, at which he asked that forgotten question. And he delicately suggests, as a matter of some urgency, a CT scan. Alarmed by what he finds, he puts me in the hands of an oncologist, who, concluding that otherwise I may be dead from cancer within a week, sets to work on me at once.

That week has been extended, but for how long? This question naturally dominates my life and the life of my family. Hope of a remission remains, though life will henceforth be very different. Nothing can be planned as a goal but only as a possibility. Again, however, as with the scandalous interview designed to ruin me, the good outweighs the bad. Never before in my life has so much appreciation come my way, and thanks to my oncologist I have been able to work at my desk, writing the report for the Commission, and organizing the Scrutopia summer school, to be taught now by friends and students.

August and September

There follow chemotherapy, intensive reading (Homer, George Eliot, Conrad, Seamus Heaney) and much intimate correspondence with friends with whom I now have no inhibitions. Marwa al-Sabouni draws my attention to the covenant between Abraham and God in its Koranic version. Hold your faith to this, she writes from Syria, but remember that your pain is your redemption. Back to *Parsifal*, by way of the Koran! And so far the pain has been a companion, but not a tyrant.

October

I am able to get out for one consoling event – the memorial service for Norman Stone, whose amused and amusing vision of modern life always cheered me. Norman was a strong defender of our inherited identity but, as a Scot, he understood that identity has many layers: a Scot is not forced to choose between being a Scot and a Brit, any more than between whisky and wine – Norman being, in the matter of alcohol, a believer in a borderless community of the Enlightened. He had a deep knowledge of the European empires, a love of Austro-Hungary and the Ottoman settlement and a remarkable acquaintance with the languages and literatures of central Europe. He set an example of imaginative involvement with other cultures that was all the more impressive for the sarcastic wit with which he punctured our patriotic illusions.

November

I am due in Prague for the 30th anniversary of the Velvet Revolution. Chemotherapy and crippled legs impede me, but Sophie's unfailing support is augmented by that of our embassy. I am now a diplomatic asset in a place where previously I rocked the boat, and the event is conducted in the highest good spirits by people grateful for the former British involvement.

Don't accept the EU propaganda version that we are celebrating the fall of the Berlin Wall as though 'freedom of movement' were all that it is about. We are celebrating the restoration of national sovereignty to people who had been absorbed and oppressed by a lawless empire. The fact that they are now absorbed by a lawful one does not alter the case.

The Czechs confer their commemorative medal on a Eurosceptic, namely me, in a touching ceremony that reminds me why, despite the appeal of the Poles, Hungarians, Romanians and many more, it is the shy, cynical Czechs to whom I lost my heart and from whom I have never retrieved it.

December

During this year much was taken from me – my reputation, my standing as a public intellectual, my position in the Conservative movement, my peace of mind, my health. But much more was given back: by Douglas Murray's generous defence, by the friends who rallied behind him, by the rheumatologist who saved my life and by the doctor to whose care I am now entrusted. Falling to the bottom in my own country, I have been raised to the top elsewhere, and looking back over the sequence of events I can only be glad that I have lived long enough to see this happen. Coming close to death you begin to know what life means, and what it means is gratitude.

Index

Afghanistan, Soviet
    invasion of 156
Althusser, Louis 80,
    143–5, 189
altruism 101–5
Alzheimer's 94
American Conservative
    37
animal rights 205–7
Arendt, Hannah 82
aristocracy 27–8
Aristotle 6, 92, 186
Arnold, Matthew
    116
Artaud, Antonin
    140
ASBOs 100
al-Assad, Hafez 48,
    169
Atatürk, Kemal 156,
    168
Austro-Hungary 230
Avicenna 14–15

Bach, J. S. 10, 217, 219
Barenboim, Daniel 24
Bauer, Peter 6
BBC 35, 48, 162, 181,
    218
Beaufort Polo
    Club 10
beauty 181–4, 217
Beethoven, Ludwig
    van 25
Benn, Tony 66, 68
Bentham, Jeremy 62
Berlin, Sir Isaiah 35
Berlin Wall, fall of
    230
Bildung 186
Blair, Cherie 14
Blair, Tony 34
Blunt, Anthony 80
Bolshevik Revolution
    168
Bosch, Hieronymus
    19

Bradley, F. H. 131
British Academy 6, 35
British Association for
    the Advancement
    of Science 4, 124
British Museum 14
British Sociological
    Association 123
Brody, Hugh 212
Brokenshire,
    James 226
Buchanan, Patrick 37
Buddha 184
Building Better,
    Building Beautiful
    Commission
    217–18, 224, 226,
    229
Burgess, Guy 80
Burke, Edmund 50–5
Bush, George W. 169

Callaghan, James 43
Cameron, David 86
Campaign for Nuclear
    Disarmament
    (CND) 6, 80
Campbell, Colin 11
Čapek, Karel 24
Čarnogurský, Ján 6, 83

Carr, E. H. 80
Carter, Jimmy 60
Charles, Prince of
    Wales 128–31
Chávez, Hugo 150–1
Chomsky, Noam 38,
    149–51
Christianity 32–3, 46,
    100, 111, 162–4, 184,
    197
    see also Easter
Christians,
    Lebanese 158–61,
    168
Churchill, Winston 49
climate change 52
Clinton, Hillary 54
communism 20, 22,
    47, 66–7, 79–82, 111,
    166
Comte, Auguste
    124–5
Conrad, Joseph 229
conservatism,
    American 37–41
Conservative
    Party 42–3, 48,
    50–3, 86, 220, 226,
    230
contraception 202

Cosmic Sausages 12

Cowling, Maurice 4

Craig-Martin,
    Michael 35

crime 31, 93, 146,
    148
    see also rape

Crimea, Russian
    invasion of 165

Czech Republic 23–4,
    219, 230

Czechoslovakia 5–6,
    19–21, 63–4, 83, 112

Dalrymple,
    Theodore 40

Darwin, Charles 99,
    109

Dawkins, Richard
    97–9

de Gaulle, Charles 49

Deleuze, Gilles 26

Derrida, Jacques 97–8

dogs, dangerous
    205

Douglas-Home,
    Charles viii

Dubček, Alexander 19,
    21

Duchamp, Marcel 25

Durkheim, Émile 110,
    124–5

Easter 220–3

Einstein, Albert
    106–7

elephants 206

Eliot, George 229

Eliot, T. S. 40

Elizabeth I, Queen 44,
    49

Elysian Singers 217

Emin, Tracey 182

European Union 14,
    21–2, 31, 167, 230

evolution 109–10,
    149

fakery 185–90

Falklands War 44

Fanshawe, Georgie 10

fascism 66–8

fasting 197

Faust 95

feminism 6, 34, 72,
    134, 194–5

Filmer, Antonia 11

fish 200–1

Foucault, Michel viii,
    139–43, 187–8

fox hunting 10–11, 14,
17–18, 27, 205–6,
211–13, 224
Franco, General
Francisco 67
Freud, Sigmund 93,
147

Gadamer, Hans-
Georg 143
Gare du Nord 218
Gellner, Ernest
148
genetic modification
94–6
Georges-Picot,
François 168
Gilbey, Monsignor
Alfred 198
Gladstone, W. E.
117
Goethe, Johann
Wolfgang von 95,
189
Golden Rule 101
Good Samaritan 101,
103–4
Gorbachev, Mikhail
165–6
Gove, Michael 45

Goya, Francisco de 97,
140
grammar schools
129–30
Gramsci, Antonio 119
Grant, Robert 195
Greer, Germaine 134,
202

Habermas, Jürgen 143
Hamrax Motors
176–7
Harvey, A. D. 7
Hašek, Jaroslav 24
Havel, Václav 6, 83, 112
Hawking, Stephen
106–7
Heaney, Seamus 229
Heath, Edward 42–3
Heath, Nicholas 11
Hegel, G. W. F. x, 62
Herbert, George 132
Hill, Christopher 80
Hirst, Damien 35, 182
Hitler, Adolf 66–7, 79
Hobsbawm, Eric 80
Hölderlin,
Friedrich 140
Homer 212, 229
Honeyford, Ray 4

Horsell's Farm
      Enterprises   28
House of Lords   69
human rights   21, 51,
      55, 59–65
Hume, Cardinal
      Basil   196
Hungary   19–20, 84,
      219, 230
hunter-gatherers   212
Hussein, Saddam
      169
Huxley, Aldous   94–5,
      202

in vitro fertilization   35
Inge, Dean   178
IRA   44
Iranian revolution   x,
      155–7
Iraq   156, 168–71
ISIS   170
Islamic law   63
Islamophobia   135, 226

James, P. D.   6
Janáček, Leoš   24, 96
Jefferson, Thomas   54
John Paul II, Pope
      20–1, 47, 124

Johnson, Boris   85–6
Jones, Rosalind   11

Kant, Immanuel
      106–8, 186, 189
Kennedy, Edward   155
KGB   83, 165–6
Khomeini, Ayatollah
      156
Kimball, Roger   40
Kinsey report   194
Kirk, Russell   40
kitsch   185
Klaus, Václav   21
Koran   164, 210, 219,
      229
Kurds   168, 170–1

Labour Party   26, 34,
      46, 52, 69–70, 205
Lacan, Jacques   189
Lascaux caves   212
Laughton, Sam   217
Lawrence, D. H.   31
Le Figaro   219, 226–7
League of Nations
      168
Leavis, F. R.   31
Lebanon   158–61
Lenin, V. I.   59, 82

Leninism 70
lesbians 35
Liverpool Cathedral 179
Locke, John 54, 62
Lorca, Federico García 227

McCarthy, Senator Joseph 79–81
Maclean, Donald 80
MacMillan, James 25
Macron, Emmanuel 227
madness 139–41
Maronite Church 158–9
Marx, Karl 43, 82, 93, 119, 124–5, 144–5, 187
Marxism 59–60, 64–5, 119–20, 144–5, 187
Matthews, David 25, 227
Mečiar, Vladimir 83
memes 97–8
Mengele, Joseph 94
Merleau-Ponty, Maurice 80
Midgley, Mary 111

Mitchison, Graeme 219
Molière 98
Mona Lisa 111
Monroe doctrine 60
Moore, Charles 46
Mozart, Wolfgang Amadeus, Don Giovanni 11–12
Mugabe, Robert 5
Muhammad, Prophet 160, 162, 169, 203–4
Murray, Douglas 226, 230
Muslims 36, 86–7, 158–60, 162–4, 169
Mussolini, Benito 66–7, 72, 125

National Economic Development Council 43
NATO 165
Nazis 82, 99
Nerval, Gérard de 140
New Criterion 40
New Right 44, 124–5
New Statesman 219–20, 225–6

Newton, Isaac   106
NHS   27, 35
Nietzsche,
	Friedrich 101, 140,
	146
Norman, Jesse   51, 53
Notre-Dame
	Cathedral 222,
	227

Oasis   11, 130
Obama, Barack
	167
Old Dominion point-
	to-point 17–18
Open University   118,
	120
Orwell, George   x
Oslzlý, Petr   24
O'Sullivan, John   47
Ottoman Empire   168,
	230
Oxford Union   45

Palestine Liberation
	Organization
	(PLO) 159
parental responsibility
	75–8
Pareto, Vilfredo   124–5

patriotism   42, 100
Pepys Show, The
	10–11
Pergolesi, Giovanni
	Battista 184
Pericles   48–9
Philby, Kim   80
Plato   6, 15
Poetics Today   123
Pol Pot   150
Poland   19–22, 47, 219,
	227–8, 230
Popiłuszko, Father   47
pornography   194–5
Powell, Enoch   42
Prague Spring   19
Prague underground
	university 26
'progress'   178–80
Proms   25
Protestantism   103
	Proust, Marcel 28
psychoanalysis   141,
	147–8, 189
public schools   71
Putin, Vladimir   165–6

Race and Religious
	Hatred Bill 162
Radio   3 31, 118

Rand, Ayn 101–4
rape 193–5
Raphael 184
rats 207
Rawls, John 37
Reading 181–2
Reagan, Ronald 44,
    47, 165, 167
Renaissance 139, 142
repair 175–7
Repin, Vadim 25
Rifkind, Malcolm 47
Rogers, Sir Richard
    (Lord Rogers of
    Riverside) 31, 35
Roman Catholic
    Church 196–8
Roman law 64
Romania 82–3, 230
Rorty, Ricahrd 188
Rousseau, Jean-
    Jacques 51, 54, 62
Rowse, A. L. 6
Royal Academy 35
Royal Orchestral
    Society 217
Ruffer, Jonathan 225
Ruskin, John 117
Russell, Bertrand x,
    143

Saatchi, Charles 182
al-Sabouni,
    Marwa 229
Sade, Marquis de 140
St Augustine 204
St John of the
    Cross 220
St Pancras station 184,
    218
St Paul 222
St Thomas Aquinas 92
Salisbury Review 3–7,
    37
Sartre, Jean-Paul 80
Saussure, Ferdinand
    de 149
Scargill, Arthur 44
Scheler, Max 124, 210
Schier, Flint 5
Schiller, Friedrich
    186
Schröder, Gerhard 166
Scott, Giles
    Gilbert 179
Searle, John 91
self-esteem 120,
    128–31
Semiotica 123
September 11
    attacks 38, 41, 151

Serota, Nicholas
182
sextants 208–9
sexting 209–10
sexual laxity 36
Seyrinx, Damien 218
Shaftesbury, Lord 117
Shakespeare,
William 228
shame 210
Slovakia 83
Smith, Adam 56, 101
Smith, Elise 12
Socialist Workers
Party 5
sociology 116, 118,
120, 124–7
Sorel, Georges 125
soul 91–3
Soviet Union, collapse
of 47, 165
Spectator 37, 225
Stalin, Josef 79, 145
Stone, Norman 229
surrogate motherhood
202–3
Sykes, Sir Mark 168
Syria 47–8, 55, 156,
158–60, 168–9, 229
Syriac language 158

telephone booths
179–80
Thatcher,
Margaret 42–9,
54, 66, 68
Theatre of the Goose
on a String 24
Themistocles
48–9
Theocritus 199
Thirty Years War 99
Tito, Marshal 80
Town and Country
Planning Acts
180
trade unions 42–4,
67–8, 196
transphobia 135
Trojan War 99
Trollope, Anthony
212
Trump, Donald
54–6

United States
Constitution 55
University of
Bradford 4, 123
University of
Buckingham 27

Van Evera, Emily
    227
Van Gogh,
    Vincent 140
Vanenburg
    Meeting 28
vegetarianism
    199
Verdi, Giuseppe 20
Viagra 95
Vichy France 66
Virgi 199
Voltaire 97

Wagner, Richard 20,
    24, 224
    Parsifal 224, 228–9
Weaver, Richard 54
Weber, Max 124–5
Weill, Kurt 11
Wilson, Harold 43
wine 8–9
women priests 31

Yugoslavia 80

Zeman, Miloš 24